Let the Little Children Come to Me

Stories of Children Martyrs

*To the young Christian martyrs
of every land and every time,
who, through their deaths,
taught us how to live.*

All biblical quotations are taken from
the New King James Version

Printed in Canada

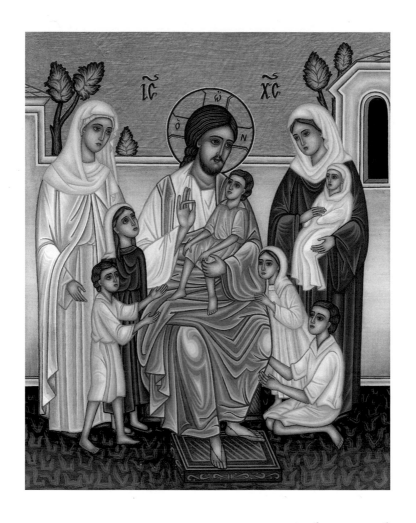

And Jesus said,
"Let the little children come to Me,
and do not forbid them,
for of such is the kingdom of heaven."

St. Matthew 19:14

Contents

Prologue

As Christ set out to establish His Church, He called forth men, women and children to assist Him in this holy labor. Planting the seeds of faith upon the earth through the missionary activities of His apostles, He watered these seeds with the blood of His martyrs. The young seedlings grew and, nurtured by millions of Christian martyrs throughout the centuries, became His Church, the mighty Tree of Life.

Children were among those chosen, for they have always been precious to the Lord and He never excluded them. In fact, it was Christ Himself Who told us that "...their angels always behold His face in the Kingdom of Heaven." Included on His holy roster of saints, they too were sanctified with crowns of martyrdom and were bestowed the honor of dwelling eternally in His Kingdom.

To those of us in the Church Militant—here on earth—the holy martyrs forever serve as witnesses to the truth of Christ's death and resurrection and as role models to a world in dire need of good examples. They followed Him in death and endured the most inhumane and horrific agonies, but did so willingly, fearlessly and joyfully, knowing without a doubt that they would share in His resurrection as He promised and be numbered among the saints.

Our first feelings when we think of martyred children may be those of sadness, for it is difficult to accept the fact that innocent children were brutalized. However, just as our Lord's agonizing crucifixion led to His glorious resurrection, so did the slaughter of His youngest of martyrs lead to glory—eternal life—"...where there is no pain, sorrow or suffering." Their stories are not narratives of death but celebrations of life.

As each of us follows his own course and faces his own pains and sorrows, the examples of the martyrs first of all remind us that our meager struggles are nothing in comparison to their great torments. Whether our "executioners" are illnesses or handicaps or poverty or abuse or temptations of any kind, we learn through the martyrs how to face them and how to emerge victorious. By their example we are shown that the only Joy, the only Hope, the only Courage, the only Strength, the only Peace, the only Truth, the only Love is Christ, our Lord and Savior. He never abandons us today, as He never abandoned His martyrs.

Although the contests of the martyrs brought their earthly death, we as children of God recognize their victory. Remaining steadfast in the faith, they gained everlasting life, and through their suffering they turned many souls to Christ, adding to His Church new branches that continue to bear fruit throughout the centuries.

In today's troubled times when the Church of Christ is bombarded by enemies from without and within, the sacrifice of these holy children shines brightly in a darkened world, attesting to the unshakable triumph of the Orthodox Christian faith, for as Christ Himself stated, "...the gates of hell shall not prevail against it." Our beloved Father, Saint John Chrysostomos, once said: "Seeing the blood of the martyrs, the angels rejoiced, the demons feared, and the devil himself trembled, because what they saw was not simply blood, but salvific blood, holy blood, blood worthy of heaven, blood which continues to nurture the holy plants of the Church."

Preface

This book began at the request of two very dear and devout women who realized the positive influence the young Christian martyrs would have on today's youth and, by God's grace, upon English-speaking Christians of all ages. It primarily includes those young Christian martyrs seventeen years of age and under who lived between the first centuries of Christianity through the early twentieth century. Though not a scholarly work by any means, much research went into its preparation.

Several obstacles presented themselves, however. First of all, this volume is not complete, for very few of the millions of martyrs through the ages are known, and of these, the ages of most have not been recorded. Also, time and space were limited, making it impossible to include the accounts of more young martyrs. I deeply regret that the stories of all cannot be told in this work, yet humbly ask for their prayers as this book goes to press.

Occasionally details vary from one *Synaxaristis* to another; often ages of saints or dates of feast days differ. Most often, however, information is limited. At other times, several saints share common names and the need to match the correct facts with the correct child-martyr presented a challenge. In such cases, I often had to use my own humble discretion. May the saints and you, the reader, forgive my errors in judgment.

My greatest obstacle, however, was my own unworthiness. Yet, through the intercessions of our loving and holy Father, Saint John Chrysostomos, who came to my aid numerous times, this labor of love and thanksgiving was completed.

It would be arrogant on my part to think that I wrote this book alone, for, as the work progressed, it became evident that it was written through the prayers of many devoted servants of God—especially through the blessings of my most pious and greatly respected Geronda and Spiritual Father, and the prayers and encouragement of my beloved Spiritual Mother to whom I am most grateful for many things.

I extend my sincerest thanks to all who contributed towards the preparation of this small volume in so many other ways. May the Lord, Who knows their sincere efforts and hard work, bless them and their families abundantly.

No names will be mentioned in this book other than the names of the holy young martyrs of God themselves, for theirs was the struggle, theirs was the faith, theirs was the victory. I thank them most of all, for they have touched my heart and will remain a part of me always.

—the author

Saint Mamas

September 2

heodotos and Rufina, a patrician couple, lived in the town of Gangra in Asia Minor in the middle of the third century during the reign of terror of Aurelian. Among the aristocracy, they were both devout Christians speaking openly about the faith and winning many souls for Christ.

News of their activities reached the ears of the tyrannical eparch Alexandros who, although enraged, refrained from taking action against them because of their status. He sent them instead to Faustus, the governor of Caesarea, who immediately ordered their imprisonment, even though Rufina was ready any day to give birth to her first child.

Theodotos and Rufina fervently prayed to the Lord: "O Christ, our King and God, stand beside us in our suffering and keep us strong so that we may never deny you. We humbly implore You to protect us for the sake of our child who will soon be born. Whatever may befall us, please keep our baby in Your care. Protect him and teach him; be with him when we cannot. Guide his footsteps that he might live for You and become a child of Light." Such were the petitions of the loving parents for the child whom they placed in God's care even before his birth.

Their prayers were heard and Rufina soon gave birth to a son in the bleak, dark prison. The parents rejoiced at his birth and thanked God for this infant, their final earthly blessing. They held him and kissed him but shortly thereafter died, leaving the tiny orphan lying between them in the prison cell.

God did not forget the child of his devoted servants and immediately sent Ammia, a good Christian woman from the area to take the infant. After burying Theodotos and Rufina in her garden, she adopted their child and raised him in the faith of his beloved parents. The boy dearly loved Ammia as his mother. When at last, at the age of five, he began to speak, the first word that he uttered was "Mama." For this reason he was given the name Mamas.

Life continued normally for the youngster. Raised as a Christian, he was set aflame with the teachings of the Lord, and with the same zeal as his parents he set out at the age of fifteen to spread the faith.

By this time the harsh idolater Democritus had replaced Faustus as governor. Upon hearing that Mamas was a Christian and had also brought others to the faith, he summoned the boy to appear before him.

"It has been brought to my attention, young man, that you are a Christian."

"I am a Christian," replied Mamas.

"Then it is my duty to inform you that you must give up this nonsense at once and turn your back on this strange sect. Otherwise, things will not go well for you," the eparch continued.

"Then it is my duty as a Christian, O Democritus, to inform you that I have no intentions of turning my back on my Lord and Savior. I am a Christian and will remain one forever," proclaimed Mamas boldly.

"I order you to sacrifice to the gods of Rome!" Democritus gruffly demanded.

"I will never sacrifice to your idols. My love and devotion belong to Christ, my Lord and my God, and to Him alone I sacrifice all that I have—including my life!"

"Then let us see just how much you are willing to sac- rifice, young man. You speak boldly but we shall soon see just how courageous you are," Democritus threat- ened. "Guards! Take care of this impudent youth!" he bellowed.

The guards seized Mamas and severely beat and tortured him. Through it all, however, the Lord protected him. Though burned with torches, his pure body remained untouched by the flames. When bound with an iron weight and tossed into the sea, an angel of the Lord delivered him from the soldiers and enabled him to find shelter in a cave atop a high mountain.

In his new home, Mamas prayed and glorified the Lord Who had come to his aid. Wild animals became his companions and sustained him with their milk. Continuing his life of prayer and teaching the faith as before, his fame quickly spread and again attracted the attention of the governor of Cappadocia, another Alexandros.

Once more he was captured and taken before the Cappadocian governor who ordered more intense tortures for him, which the boy endured patiently and courageously. Born in a prison to Christian parents, he was not afraid to die for Christ. Amidst his suffering, Mamas was encouraged by the voice of His Lord and Savior, Jesus Christ, a miraculous phenomenon heard by many Christians witnessing his martyrdom. "Rejoice Mamas, my child, for I will always be with you."

Enraged by the lad's steadfastness to his faith and determined to break his resolve, the tyrant had Mamas thrown into prison; but there, impounded with other Christian captives, the youth prayed for their release. Miraculously, the doors of the prison opened and all escaped. Only Mamas remained, accompanied and strengthened by an angel of the Lord.

Alexandros ordered more torment for him, yet, by the mercy of God, a fiery furnace did not burn him. Ferocious beasts only knelt before him. Embarrassed and furious at his defeat, the ruler ordered that he be taken out of the city and executed. So it was that Mamas was bound and led out of the city where he was stabbed with a three-pronged spear. Despite this fatal blow, the young martyr found his way to a cave where his last breath was spent in prayer to his Lord Who had guided and protected him since birth. He joyfully took his place among the righteous on September 2nd, the day on which the Church commemorates his blessed memory.

Saint Vasilissa of Nicomedia

September 3

During the diabolical reign of the Emperor Diocletian, the blood of Christian martyrs soaked the land. Among the countless Saints of Christ slaughtered during this time was Saint Vasilissa, who received the crown of martyrdom at a tender age.

Arrested and brought before Alexandros, the governor of Nicomedia, Vasilissa showed boldness and wisdom beyond her mere ten years. Neither flattery nor threat of torture could force her to deny her faith in Christ.

When Alexandros realized that Vasilissa remained unmoved, he ordered that harsh torments be inflicted upon her youthful body. Flogging, thrashing, piercing, hanging—she heroically endured all. Alexandros became wild with rage and ordered that she be thrown into a furnace. Instead of witnessing her death, however, all present testified how she had remained untouched by the flames. She was then thrown into a den of lions, but the Lord miraculously closed the mouths of the wild beasts and she was unharmed.

The governor was greatly bewildered by the unexpected turn of events and, enlightened by the mercy of the Almighty God, fell at the girl's feet. "O young maiden of God, please forgive the evil actions of the great sinner who now kneels before you. I have been blind all my life without even knowing that I could not see; I have been deaf, but knew not my deafness. Now, however, through your sufferings, the Lord has opened my eyes that I might see the path that leads to Him. He has opened my ears that I might hear His voice calling me to repentance. I have seen His great power, His great strength and

His great love, and I long to be numbered among His chosen servants. Will He accept me now, after all the suffering I have inflicted upon you, his young child?"

Vasilissa, despite all that she had endured, was filled with joy at God's unlimited mercy. Looking up to heaven, her face shone radiantly as she prayed: "I thank You, my sweetest Jesus, for the great mercy You have shown Alexandros this day. Forgive his every sin and accept him as Your devoted servant. Thank You for allowing me to suffer in Your most holy Name that the eyes of this man might be opened to the truth."

Soon after, Vasilissa left the city and found a rock upon which she rested from her long ordeal. By now she was exhausted and prayed for water to quench her great thirst. Immediately, water gushed forth from the rock upon which she rested and upon which she had humbly prayed. Falling to her knees and thanking God for helping her endure her torments, she surrendered her tender soul to her Lord and Savior.

Saints Urbanus, Prilidianus and Epolonius

(with Saint Babylas, Bishop of Antioch)

September 4

aints Urbanus, Prilidianus and Epolonius were the spiritual children and students of the pious Babylas, Bishop of Antioch. It was the year 283 A.D, a time when Christians were tortured and slaughtered in the most brutal ways possible.

Numerianos, the ruler at the time, was an evil man who participated in demonic rituals and sacrifices. His regard for human life was minimal and his concern for Christians even less. One day he decided to enter a Christian church. It was the holy day of Pascha, and his mere presence would defile the holy place of worship—especially since he had just participated in demonic rituals, which included sacrificing the King of Persia's young son to the idols. Babylas, the Bishop of Antioch, would not tolerate the defilement of God's holy temple by anyone and met Numerianos at the door of the church, barring his entry. The ruler was furious but, fearing the people, left without making a scene.

The next day he summoned Babylas to appear before him. "How dare you, Babylas, forbid me, your king, to enter your church!" he raged. "I am the ruler here and my word is law! I have an order for you now, in fact," he deviously smiled. "If you bow down before the mighty gods of Rome and worship them, then I might forgive your actions of yesterday. If you refuse, then, I warn you, many torments await you!"

Babylas could not be threatened and boldly responded, "The gods of Rome are far from mighty. Only one God reigns and He is the only God, the one I worship, the one to Whom I pledge my life. Look at your man-made idols, O king, and you will see no life in them. They are lifeless because they are false; they are powerless before my God because they are demons. The God of the Christians is the living God. Look about you and see what He has created. Ask Him to open the eyes of your soul and you will see that what I am telling you is true. My God offers peace and love; yours, violence and hatred. Mine offers salvation; yours, eternal damnation. Come with me to my church in repentance and you will be changed forever."

"Enough of your babbling, old man," Numerianos interrupted. "Either you worship my gods or you will regret that you refused my offer."

"You are wasting your time," the bishop replied, "for I will never turn away from the Lord God to worship demons. I have served Christ all my life and will continue to do so until the day I die!"

"Then die you will!" Numerianos shouted, leaping to his feet. "Bring the iron chains," he commanded his soldiers. "Fasten them tightly around his neck and legs and parade him through the streets! We will see what the Christians will think of their bishop in chains!" he sneered. The holy bishop stood up straight and looked into the ruler's eyes. "I thank you for my chains, O king, for they symbolize my servitude to Christ, my Savior. I value them as dearly as you value your royal garments and imperial crown."

Watching the proceedings were the three young brothers, Urbanus, Prilidianus and Epolonius who had refused to leave their beloved teacher. Though only twelve, nine and seven years old, the boys were spiritually wise beyond their years. When Numerianos asked about the boys' identities, Babylas related that they were his spiritual children who were divinely inspired by the true God of the Christians.

The boys' mother was immediately dragged before the king. Stating that her name was Christodouli, she affirmed that she had offered her sons to the Lord God by way of Bishop Babylas who, she was certain, would help them enter the Kingdom of Heaven. Angered by her response, Numerianos ordered his servants to strike her repeatedly, all the while abusing her verbally, as well.

Witnessing their mother's beatings, the boys loudly shouted. "You are a madman, evil king! Our mother speaks the truth! Why do you beat her for this?"

In a rage, Numerianos turned against the brothers and ordered that each be harshly beaten. Twelve-year-old Urbanus received twelve thrashings; nine-year-old Prilidianus received nine and seven-year-old Epolonius received seven. But the young lads endured their torments and praised God for giving them the opportunity to suffer in His Name.

Babylas was brought forth again. "Your three young students have just agreed to worship the gods of Rome," the ruler tempted him. "Don't you think you should follow their lead and do the same?"

Babylas, however, the divinely inspired servant of God, correctly perceived the king's deception. "You are lying, sir," he said. "My students would never worship demons. They love Christ as much as I do and would never turn against Him."

The vile emperor exploded with fury! He commanded the most brutal tortures be given to the three boys and their teacher. The loving spiritual father prayed for his children, asking God to help them endure until the end. All four were hung and tormented by fire, but despite their agony the young brothers gazed upon the face of their beloved teacher and spiritual father with joy. Through his prayers they were strengthened.

When they were finally taken down, the boys remained calm and unaffected. Numerianos tried again to entice them—this time with flattery and promises of great wealth—but, once more, his words failed to sway them. Instead, they reaffirmed their commitment to Christ more emphatically.

The pious bishop heard their sincere declarations of faith and lifted his eyes in prayer. "My Christ," he began, "I thank you for Urbanus, Prilidianus and Epolonius, the young students you have given me, and for the privilege of guiding their footsteps along the road of salvation. Thank you for letting my humble teachings fall upon fertile soil. And now, I beseech You to stand beside them in their suffering and lead them into Your Kingdom."

Enraged that an old bishop and three small boys had defeated him, Numerianos sentenced them to death by the sword. The three young brothers and their teacher were led to the place of execution. To insure that they would not turn away in fear, Babylas sent the boys ahead of him. Awaiting death, he reminded them of the great rewards that God had prepared for them. As they approached the executioner one by one, Babylas cried out the words of the Prophet Isaiah: "Here am I and the children whom the Lord has given me!" With these last words, holy Babylas, the saintly bishop, spiritual father and teacher, followed his beloved students into martyrdom.

At his request, devout Christians buried the hierarch with the chains that had bound him throughout his trials. The three holy brothers were buried beside him. But this was not the end for them. Together they had given up their souls and passed over to a new beginning in the Kingdom of Heaven.

Saints Ammonios, Donatos and Eighty-Two Other Children

(with Saint Babylas)

September 4

he year 298 A.D, under the Emperor Maximianos, was a time of great persecution for Christians. Despite the danger, however, the followers of Jesus Christ continued to multiply. Christians met secretly to worship and also to be instructed in the faith. Such were the circumstances for eighty-four children who met secretly to learn the teachings of Christ from their elderly teacher Babylas.

One day idolaters approached Maximianos with news of an elderly man who taught a group of children about Jesus, the Crucified One. The emperor immediately dispatched soldiers to arrest the man and his students and to bring them before him for questioning.

Standing before the emperor, Babylas was calm as his interrogation began. The emperor was not impressed by the man who stood before him. It would be easy to win him over, he thought. After all, he was just a tired, old man. The questioning began.

"Are you Babylas, the teacher?"

"Yes, I am called Babylas, and by the grace of God, I am a Christian and a teacher."

Maximianos smirked, "So, you are a follower of this Jesus Who was crucified. I see," he nodded, rubbing his chin. "How can you, old man, worship a God Who is dead? Why…just look at our wonderful Roman gods. Aren't they grand? Why don't you worship them instead? After all, the citizens of Rome all honor them…..

And, these children you teach…how can you teach them about this Jesus and not tell them about Rome's finest deities?"

Babylas, who had been standing quietly, was now ready to speak. Looking first at the bright faces of his young students, he turned to face the emperor.

"You ask many things, O emperor. You are indeed a ruler, but you know nothing. If you are a great ruler, why don't you know the greatness of the one true God, the God Who is very much alive and not dead as you think Him to be? You ask why I teach my students about Christ. A teacher is obligated to teach the truth, and there is no truth without God. The Roman gods are false; they are the lies of the father of lies himself—the devil. It is not logical, O Maximianos, that a teacher would teach lies instead of truth. It is not logical that a Christian should speak of demons instead of the Lord God. I pity you, Maximianos. You may be emperor, but you are blinded by your power. You are blinded by your wealth. You are blinded by your overwhelming pride. One who is blind cannot see the truth."

Maximianos was infuriated by the teacher's bold reply and commanded his solders to pelt him with stones. The torments began.

Babylas faced his punishment joyfully. Covered with blood, he thanked God for allowing him, a sick, old man, to be tortured for Him. Continuing to beat him, the soldiers tied heavy chains around his neck and threw him into prison where his legs were placed in wooden stocks.

With Babylas out of the way, Maximianos turned his attention to the children, trying with flattery to coax them into worshipping the idols. When the youngsters would not be swayed, the ruler took ten of the older children aside.

"I have selected you ten from among the others because I can tell by your faces that you are not only older but wiser, as well," he began, attempting to flatter them into submission. "A wise person would understand what I am saying and seize the opportunity I am about to offer. Is not the splendor of Rome great? Wouldn't you like to have gold and silver, lavish meals and fine clothing?" he asked, flashing his golden rings with precious stones before their eyes. "Wouldn't you like a few of these trinkets for yourselves?" he grinned haughtily. All of these fine things can be yours, my children, if you will only forget this Jesus, this Nazarene, and accept the imperial gods of Rome. Well, what do you say, my children?"

Ammonios and Donatos, as spokesmen for the children, stepped forward. "First of all, O emperor, we are not your children. We are all children of our Lord Jesus Christ. Do not think even for a moment that because we are young we are impressed by your wealth or intimidated by the power of Rome. Our wealth is our God and we would never turn from Him. We speak for all of our spiritual brothers and sisters in the Lord that stand beside us in this room. Our God is the one and only God and we would rather be tortured than sacrifice to the demons of Rome which you ignorantly worship."

Their impassioned declaration of faith filled Maximianos with rage and he ordered his soldiers to beat the children; but instead of cowering, they withstood their torments bravely, all the while proclaiming their devotion to Jesus Christ, their Lord and God, Whom they would never deny. The brutal emperor commanded in a fury that they be beaten even more severely and thrown into prison where, denied food and water, they would either renounce their Christian God or starve to death. Babylas was ordered to be hung up and severely beaten.

Once more Maximianos pressured the children, "Because I am a kind man, I give you one last chance to renounce this Christ of yours and your deluded old teacher."

"Nothing you can say or offer will change our minds," the children replied. "Kill us quickly, O emperor, that we might soon be united with our beloved Lord."

For their refusal to obey the evil emperor's demands, all eighty-four children, with their beloved Babylas, were sentenced to death by beheading. Devout Christians collected the holy relics of the children and their teacher by night, and took them by boat to Constantinople, where they were buried outside the city walls at the Monastery of Chora.

Saints Pistis, Elpis and Agape

(with Saint Sofia)

September 17

During the second century when the Emperor Hadrian, a zealous idolater, occupied the throne, a young widow of noble birth named Sofia lived in Rome with her three daughters. A devout Christian, Sofia (which means wisdom) named her daughters Pistis (Faith), Elpis (Hope) and Agape (Love) after the three great Christian virtues. As beautiful as they were outwardly, so much more beautiful were they inwardly, for the Church of Christ was for them not just a set of rules but indeed, as it should be, a way of life. Along with their daily chores, they spent much time in prayer and in acquiring greater knowledge of God.

As they grew in wisdom and in the fear of God, their fame spread also and soon reached the ears of the eparch Antiochus, who wished to see them for himself. He was extremely upset because the family had not only embraced but also exemplified the Christian ideals, so he reported them to the emperor. Hadrian was enraged and commanded that Sofia and her offspring be brought to trial.

Sofia realized, without a doubt, what this summons meant and prepared her children for the contest that would soon begin. They were still so young. She had raised them alone after the death of her husband, and with the Lord's guidance and blessings, she had reared them as God-fearing Christians. Now that faith would be tested. Sofia was not afraid, however, for she had placed her trust in Christ as she had always done during times of strife and had instilled this same trust in her children.

She called them together. "My beloved daughters, the greatest joys of my earthly life, you know that we have been summoned to appear before the emperor. Our trials may be great—eventually leading to our deaths. The path we are about to take ends in defeat and death for those who do not know Christ. For those of us who know Him, it ends in victory and eternal life. I do not know what awaits us; but, this I know: Our Lord and Savior Jesus Christ will stand beside us all the way. He will give us strength to endure whatever torments we might encoun-

ter. Remember, my darlings, physical pain lasts momentarily; the Kingdom of God lasts forever. We must be patient and courageous to gain that eternal glory. We must surrender our lives to His care and never fear. Cling tightly to Him. Pray to Him. Ask for His help and our merciful God will come to our aid as He always has."

Pistis, Elpis and Agape kissed and embraced their mother. "Don't be afraid, dearest Mother," they reassured her. "We will remember your words and pray that our Lord will keep all of us strong so that we may enter His kingdom together." After offering a final prayer, they joined their hands together and set out to face whatever lay before them.

At the palace of the emperor, Sofia was brought alone before the malicious Hadrian who marveled at her boldness and wisdom. When he saw that all efforts to coax her into renouncing her faith were futile, he sent for the three young sisters. However, he fared no better with them, for they shared the same love for Christ as their mother and no prodding on his part could alter their sincere and pure devotion to Christ.

Nevertheless, before passing judgment upon them, Hadrian decided to try a different approach. A certain noblewoman named Palladia was assigned to them for three days in order to teach them the ways of the idolaters. Rather than follow Palladia's directives, Sofia instead spent the time encouraging her daughters to face the certain martyrdom that awaited them.

After three days when Sofia and her children were returned to the emperor, Hadrian proceeded to entice the girls with promises of riches and a life of ultimate luxury and esteem. Little did he understand that, despite their youth, Pistis, Elpis and Agape had no interest whatsoever in an earthly kingdom but had set their eyes on the Heavenly Kingdom. Not even threats of agonizing torture could alter their conviction.

Each of the girls was then called individually for inter-rogation. Pistis, the eldest, was first. Encouraged by the prayers of her beloved mother and sisters, she faced Hadrian.

"You as the oldest must also be the wisest," Hadrian said to the girl, hoping to win her over with flattery. "Therefore, you must make your sisters realize the error of their ways. Convince them to turn their backs upon Jesus, the carpenter of Nazareth, and to accept the great gods of Rome and I will shower you with great wealth. Come now, my child, just sacrifice to the goddess Artemis. What harm can it do to make your emperor happy?"

Pistis calmly responded, "O Hadrian, you are only an earthly ruler. My God rules the universe. He is the only one my sisters and I will serve. Your Artemis is no god-dess at all. She is only a lifeless idol and I will never bow down before her."

"Are you aware, young girl, that I have the power to torture you, to mutilate you and to kill you?" he screamed, his face turning a bright crimson.

"You can only kill my body, O emperor. My spirit belongs to God, and by His great mercy it will live for-ever with Him in heaven."

Hadrian was deeply shaken. Things were not going as he had expected. First he had confronted Sofia's obstina-cy, now her daughter's. It was time to apply pressure.

Sofia, Elpis and Agape watched as their beloved Pistis was beaten severely. They prayed for her as the twelve-year-old was mutilated and burned. By God's grace, Pistis was not harmed. Throughout her trials, she re-mained joyful and peaceful, anticipating the heavenly crown that awaited her. Finally, in front of her beloved family, she was beheaded.

Next, Elpis was brought forth. The same line of ques-tioning occurred, followed by deceitfully gentle coaxing and then by harsh threats.

"Young lady," he stated firmly, "you have just witnessed the suffering and death of your oldest sister. Is this what you want also? Be reasonable. I can free you or slaughter you. Which shall it be?"

"You offer no worthy choice, O emperor," Elpis replied. "I am a Christian and my heart and soul belong to My Lord, Jesus Christ, Whom I long to see. I do not fear the physical torments. My Christ is standing beside me guiding my way."

"Very well, then," Hadrian said, pounding his fist on his throne. "Let us see if your God will come to your aid."

Hadrian underestimated the power of true Christian faith. Despite the horrendous tortures—the beatings, the burning, the hanging, the lacerating of her flesh with iron claws—the ten-year-old maiden's faith and love for the Lord remained firm. During her savage ordeal her face shone brilliantly and her body emitted a sweet fragrance to the wonder of all present. Instead of cowering in fear, she rejoiced, knowing that she would soon stand before Christ, the Lord. When the order for her own beheading was given, she willingly offered her neck for the sake of His Kingdom.

In turn, nine-year-old Agape came forward. "Surely," the tyrant thought, "I can change the mind of this mere wisp of a girl, so innocent and helpless."

"Child, you have seen what happens to those who refuse to follow the orders of mighty Rome. This is madness! Choose more wisely than your foolish sisters have. After all, your mother should be left with at least one daughter in her old age."

"Don't worry about my mother, O Hadrian," Agape courageously answered. "She is a wise and God-fearing woman and rejoices that her daughters are with our Lord. I long to be with them also. Don't waste your words."

Overwhelmingly angry and embarrassed that three small girls had defeated him, the emperor ordered even harsher tortures for Agape. But Christ stood beside her as He had with Pistis and Elpis. She was beaten; she was hanged; her body was stretched and dislocated, but with God's help she endured all.

As the holy child remained alive despite the horrendous suffering imposed upon her, the command was issued to hurl Agape into a fiery furnace. Hearing the royal decree, Agape did not wait to be thrown in, but fearlessly she walked into the furnace voluntarily. The flames consumed many pagans watching the spectacle; the cruel despot himself suffered burns. However, Agape's body remained untouched by the fire and she praised God Who had used her to reveal His mighty power before the idolaters. The little girl endured more agony when her entire body was pierced with sharp skewers. Finally, she too was beheaded. Sofia rejoiced and glorified God for bestowing upon her cherished daughters the holy crowns of martyrdom. Taking up their sacred and most precious relics, she reverently buried them together. With the heart of a mother she wept upon their graves for three days before she, committing her soul into the hands of God, was reunited with her loving family before the throne of God.

The Lord placed the crown of a martyr upon her head also, for although she did not suffer physical pain, she suffered within her heart the agony that only a mother could know witnessing the struggles of her children. On the seventeenth of September the Church remembers Pistis, Elpis, Agape and Sofia—the love of a mother and her children—and their endless devotion to Jesus Christ, the Savior.

Saint Rais

September 23

About the end of the third century at Tamman, Egypt, there lived a Christian priest named Peter who was blessed with a beautiful daughter whom he loved dearly. Spending much time with her father, Rais, from an early age, embraced the faith and her heart was set aflame with the love of Christ.

As her love for the Lord grew, Rais desired with all her heart to devote her life to Christ by entering the monastic life. Realizing his child's great piety and love, Father Peter joyfully agreed, blessed the twelve-year-old and sent her to the women's monastery at Tamman.

One day, as she accompanied other nuns to the well to draw water, she saw a group of Christians who had been arrested by the tyrant Loukianos. Priests and deacons, monks and nuns, they were treated cruelly and abused both verbally and physically.

Rais stepped forward boldly. "What great crime have these righteous people committed that you treat them so harshly?" she asked.

The guards were startled by her courageous request. How could one so young dare to confront them?

Rais asked again, "What crime have they committed? Look how shamefully you treat them."

The men laughed at her request but replied, "They have been arrested because they are Christians. They follow the sect of the Crucified One. Their kind are banned by the state, you know. So since they refuse to deny their Jesus, they will probably be sentenced to death."

"Then I will die with them," said Rais joyfully, "for I am also a Christian and will happily die for my Lord."

"But you're just a child. Get out of here now and I'll forget that I ever heard you say those words," said one of the guards who had compassion on the young girl. "Leave quickly!"

"I will not leave, kind sir," she emphatically stated. "I am a Christian and I shall die with my brothers and sisters in Christ. If the state says that Christians must be put to death, then I must die also. Now tie me up with the others," she insisted.

Rais was taken prisoner along with the other Christians. She did not cower; neither did she exhibit any signs of fear as she stood face to face with Loukianos and refused to deny her Lord and Savior.

Loukianos paced back and forth. His contempt for the Christians was great. The more he heard the Christian prisoners confess their faith and proclaim the name of the Savior, the angrier he became. Finally, in a rage, he shouted, "I spit upon the Christian God!"

Young Rais did not hesitate for a minute. She fearlessly stepped up to Loukianos. "I will never let anyone speak of my Heavenly Father with such contempt!" And, having spoken those words, she spat in the ruler's face.

Loukianos was filled with rage. He ordered that the young nun be tortured immediately. Rais, however, did not regret her actions and faced her torments willingly and gallantly. She was filled with joy as she anticipated her entrance into the Kingdom of Heaven and stood courageously as the command to behead her was issued. She voluntarily offered her life to the Lord from Whom she received the crown of martyrdom. By being steadfast and loyal to the end, she now rejoices with her companions in His realm of eternal bliss.

Saint Nicholas
the New Martyr

September 23

n Karpenissi, Greece, in 1657, a son was born to devout Christian parents and given the name Nicholas. A pious and respectful boy, Nicholas learned the Christian teachings at Karpenissi before being taken by his father to Constantinople to assist him in his grocery business.

Across from the family's grocery store was a Turkish barber, a friend of Nicholas' father. Because the barber was educated, the father asked him to teach his son the Turkish language to enable him to deal with the Turkish population more effectively. As the lessons progressed, the barber became so impressed with the boy's love of letters and his nobility of stature that he secretly vowed to convert the fifteen-year-old to the Moslem religion and conspired with fellow Turks to set a trap for him.

One day when Nicholas arrived at the barbershop for his lessons, the cunning teacher was ready to set his plan into motion. Handing the young student his reading assignment for the day, he purposely failed to reveal to him its contents. Nicholas began reciting his lessons loudly as the barber had always directed him to do. However, the boy didn't know that what he was reading was actually the Moslem creed of faith. As he read it, the barber's friends entered the shop, as planned. When the boy's recitation was over, the devious Turks joyfully declared, "Congratulations, Nicholas, you are now a Moslem!"

Nicholas was startled by their statement. "You must be mistaken. I am not Moslem; I am a Christian," he retorted.

"No, boy," they repeated, "you are now a Moslem, for you have just recited the Moslem confession of faith."

"No, you are wrong," insisted Nicholas. "What I have recited was only my lesson. I didn't know that it was the Moslem confession of faith. If I had realized, I wouldn't have read it. I was only told by my teacher to read my assignment, and that is exactly what I did. I am a Christian and will remain a Christian forever! I will never renounce my Christ to become a Moslem!"

Nevertheless, the evil plotters were determined to convert the lad. Paying no heed to the boy's protests, they took him by force to the Turkish authorities where false witnesses were prepared to attest that Nicholas had willingly read the Moslem declaration of faith in their presence.

When the government officials asked the boy if the charges brought against him were true, Nicholas fearlessly defended himself. "No, they are not true. I have been taking lessons from the barber at my father's request so that I might learn the Turkish language for business reasons. The barber tricked me. I have not mastered the language yet, and so I didn't know what I was reading, since my teacher didn't tell me what it was. After my recitation, these men entered and said that I was a Moslem. I will tell you now as I told them then—I have no intentions of converting to Islam. My Christ is the true God, the only God, the Maker of heaven and earth, and I will love Him always. I will never exchange the light for the darkness. I will never leave the truth for a lie."

The official stared at Nicholas in amazement. Never before had he heard such boldness and eloquence from one so young. Although he realized that the barber had deceived the youth, he nevertheless sided with his comrades.

"That will be enough, young man!" the official said. "The fact still remains that you did indeed recite the

Moslem confession of faith. According to our law, that makes you a Moslem!"

The government representative then softened his tone momentarily in an attempt to lure Nicholas to the Islamic side. "You have a lot to gain, young man. Don't be such a zealot. What have the Christians offered you? Nothing! We offer you countless riches and any position among our ranks that you desire. As a young man, you will have many years ahead of you to advance into the top positions of our land. Don't you see the benefits? You are a bright lad. You must think of your future and not waste your time on these lofty ideals of yours. They will get you nowhere. Be reasonable now and say that you are a Moslem."

As the Turk spoke, Nicholas recalled Jesus' temptation in the wilderness when the devil offered him all the kingdoms of the world. How appropriately it fit his situation now. Standing before the official, the boy replied, "I have already given you my answer. Do you think I am impressed with your gifts of wealth and glory? Only a shallow person would think that material possessions could be a substitute for eternal life. No matter how much you offer me, I will ALWAYS be a Christian! I will never deny my Lord! My Christ offers me more than you will ever know. He offers me salvation and a place in His Kingdom forever. You are wasting your time because I will never leave my Lord and Savior!"

Realizing the young Christian's unwavering faith, the Turks tied him to a pole, attempting to frighten him into submission with threats of torture. But nothing would sway Nicholas.

"Your wicked threats do not frighten me. Your torments will not change my beliefs. To suffer for Christ is a great honor for me, His unworthy child, and I welcome the opportunity you have given me to lay down my life for Him."

The devious Turks still refused to concede. Their goal was to force him to accept Mohammed. They even went so far as to circumcise the boy to prove that he indeed followed the tenets of Islam. In spite of this, Nicholas would not budge. His faith and love for Christ were deeply ingrained within his entire being. He loved Him more than his own life.

Filled with rage, the Moslem Turks threw the lad into prison, where he remained for sixty-five days in the company of hardened criminals. But Nicholas used his time wisely, preparing for his impending death. His days and nights were spent in prayer, and by the grace of the Almighty he remained strong in body and spirit. When brought before the authorities again, he was in good health and his face radiated an angelic serenity and brilliance.

One last time the Moslems insisted upon the youth's conversion and once more he refused. Furious at their defeat, the Turks again imprisoned him and beat him relentlessly until his body was covered with wounds.

Then Nicholas was visited by a wealthy Turk who offered a different approach. Joining his countrymen in their efforts to convert the boy, he offered unlimited wealth, gifts and even his daughter's hand in marriage. Nicholas remained firm. His wealth was his God and no material wealth could compare to this treasure.

When all the Turks' efforts failed to convince the boy to deny Christ, he was sentenced to death by beheading. Nicholas remained fearless and joyous and warmly greeted Christians he encountered along the way to his execution. With eyes and heart turned heavenward, the lad fervently prayed to the Lord, thanking Him for making him worthy to die a martyr's death.

After the execution, Nicholas' body remained unburied for three days. Both Christians and non-Christians beheld a holy light that shone around the

young martyr those three days. Finally, he was buried at
the Monastery of Panagia at Halki by pious Christians
who were required to pay for permission to take him to
his final resting-place. Today his sacred skull and relics
rest at Mount Athos at the Monastery of Xeropotamou
where they continue to heal the Christian faithful.

Saint Peter the Aleut

September 24

hen Alaska was under the Russian flag, there lived at Kodiak Island in the early 1800s a young Aleut native named Cungagnaq. When he was baptized by Russian Orthodox hieromonk missionaries, he was given the Christian name Peter.

In 1815, fourteen-year-old Peter accompanied thirteen other fur traders who had been sent on an expedition by the Russian-American Company. However, when they approached California, Spanish sailors looted their ship, and all fourteen on board were taken as prisoners to San Francisco. In the prison Peter was locked in a cell with a man named Kychaly. Separated from the others, these two endured even greater trials.

The next day a Roman Catholic priest entered their cell with several Indians. "I have come to you," the priest began, "because I am a compassionate man and want to help you see the error of your ways. You have been taken as prisoners because you have dared to enter our waters. But I am concerned about you because of your erroneous beliefs. Are you willing to accept the beliefs of the Roman Catholic Church?" he asked them, getting right to the point.

"We are Orthodox Christians, members of the Church of Christ and will never leave the truth."

"You don't know what you are saying, young man," the priest continued. "If you join us, you will join what is good and righteous."

Young Peter looked at the Jesuit priest with no sign of fear. Instead, he pitied him for his inability to clearly understand the teachings of Christ.

"You claim to be a compassionate man and speak to me of goodness and righteousness, yet your actions do not convey these virtues. How does a man who claims to be a Christian and a man of God justify such acts?"

The priest was taken aback by Peter's boldness. "I demand that you join the Roman Catholics! If you refuse to do so willingly, then perhaps my companions here will be able to convince you under torture. Does that appeal to you, young man?"

"Do what you will to me," the boy replied. "I am not afraid. I am an Orthodox Christian by the grace of God, and I will never leave my beloved Church, the true Church of Christ."

The priest continued taunting and threatening the two men. He was determined to prevail. Motioning to his men, he ordered, "See if you can help this one here with the sharp tongue change his mind first," he said, pointing to Peter.

The men seized the young Aleut, and at the priest's command they proceeded to cut off his fingers and toes, one joint at a time. When that order had been methodically carried out, the young man's hands and feet were also amputated. Peter prayed for strength to endure his suffering for the sake of his beloved Lord and His Kingdom.

"Are you ready now to renounce your faith?" the priest snarled. Haven't you had enough?"

Peter remained silent. The end of his earthly life was near and he was determined to die as an Orthodox Christian. Finally, the priest ordered that the boy be disemboweled. In excruciating pain with his blood covering the ground, Peter, the devout Orthodox Christian, received the holy crown of victory and entered the Kingdom of Heaven, thus becoming the first Native American to be enlisted among the sacred ranks of martyrs.

Kychaly and the other prisoners were to suffer the same tortures the following day. However, during the night an order from Monterrey arrived, demanding the immediate release of the captives. The next morning all were freed. Only the relics of the young martyred Aleut remained. His gravesite is unknown but is believed to be at an Indian cemetery at the Mission Delores.

In 1980, Peter, the young Native American, was canonized by the Church and is remembered each year on September 24th. As Saint Herman of Alaska prayed when he heard the account of Saint Peter's martyrdom, we also, in seeking his intercession, remember his words: "Holy, newly martyred Peter, pray to God for us!"

Saints Sevinianos, Maximos, Rufus and Evgenios

(with Saints Paul and Tatti)

September 25

Very little is known of Saints Sevinianos, Maximos, Rufus and Evgenios who were martyred with their parents, Paul and Tatti, at Damascus, their hometown. After embracing the Christian faith, the devout family set out to spread the Gospel of Christ to all who would listen.

As news of their actions reached the pagan rulers, the six were thrown into prison where their legs were placed in irons. For refusing to deny their faith, they were severely beaten and placed upon one of the cruelest instruments of torture, which stretched and twisted their bodies, causing excruciating suffering and a slow, agonizing death. Courageous to the end, the four children and their parents received the crowns of martyrdom from the Lord for Whom they had given their lives. The Church honors their victory and their entry into the heavenly realm on September 25th.

Saint Aquilina
the New Martyr

September 27

In the town of Zagliveri in northern Greece lived a man named George with his devout Christian wife and their young daughter Aquilina. One day as he argued with a Turk in the village, the dispute accelerated into a violent brawl which ended with George's stabbing and killing him. Upon hearing the news, other Turks immediately seized George and sentenced him to death.

George, however, was weak and, rather than face an agonizing death, gave into their demands and became a Moslem. He was not only freed but also showered with great riches and gifts by the Turks who considered the winning of a Christian to Islam a great victory.

George's wife and daughter, however, were pierced to the heart upon learning that George had denied Christ and, with other Christians, they mourned his fate. No amount of coaxing on their part could make him return to the true faith, for he was blinded by the wealth and praises of the Moslems.

The devout wife and mother, nevertheless, continued living the Christian life and raised her only child accordingly. Aquilina was a pious girl. As the years progressed, so did her love for Christ increase. He was the Lord and Savior and she knew that she would cling to Him forever.

In time, the Turks began putting demands on George regarding his child. "George," they emphatically stated, "your daughter Aquilina is growing rapidly. It is time that she follows your example and becomes a Moslem. You, as her father, are obliged to see that she makes this decision as soon as possible, for her sake as well as for yours."

George had grown accustomed to the new lifestyle he was living. For him things of the flesh had superceded the things of the spirit and he lived the secular life of delusion. Afraid to lose his newly acquired gifts, he confronted his daughter.

"Aquilina, it is time for you to renounce your Christian ties and become a Moslem. You will have a good life as a Moslem. Look at me—I have money, I have honor, I have a good position..."

"You have nothing, father," Aquilina responded before her father could finish his sentence. "You speak only of superficial things, material things—things that mean nothing to me. I will never become a Moslem as you have."

"But, child," continued George, "you are bright and very reasonable. Surely you must recognize a good opportunity when you see it. I know for a fact that if you renounce your faith, you will be given the pasha's son for a husband. Just think what that would mean to our family!"

"I pity you, my father," Aquilina said sadly, "for you are losing your soul for the sake of money and rank. I am deeply saddened by your inability to see the truth. My mother and all of our Christian friends mourn your blindness. You will never win me over to your greedy, empty lifestyle!"

George was enraged by his daughter's response. When all attempts failed to convince the fifteen-year-old, he resorted to violence. His love for her turned to hate and he began abusing her both verbally and physically. Although he beat her, starved her and locked her up, Aquilina remained fearless and would never concede. Finally her father turned her over to the Turkish Moslems for further punishment.

Aquilina's mother was heartbroken as she thought of the torments that awaited her beautiful child; but, as a true Christian mother, she prepared Aquilina for the trials that lay ahead and encouraged her to remain firm in the faith. She reminded her of the glorious crown awaiting her in Christ's Kingdom if she endured to the end.

Leaving the tender embrace of her beloved mother, Aquilina was taken before the Turkish leaders. She boldly faced them and courageously pledged eternal love for Jesus Christ, the only King and God.

Realizing all too quickly that Aquilina's strength and

courage far surpassed her father's and that she could never be won over to their side, the Turks immediately stripped off her clothing and beat her mercilessly with sticks and metal rods. Her young body became one massive wound, while her blood flowed to the ground like a river. Through it all, she remained true to her Lord; born a Christian, she would die a Christian!

After three days of brutal torture, Aquilina was taken home to the arms of her mother who had never ceased praying for her precious child. Uncertain why Aquilina had been allowed to return home, she approached the severely wounded girl cautiously.

"My child, what have you done? Why have you been returned to your home? Have you given in to the Turkish demands, my daughter? Have you denied our Christ?" she asked tearfully, almost afraid to hear her answer. She had wept so bitterly over her husband's denial of the faith that it would be unbearable for her if her daughter should lose her soul also. She looked at her and softly stroked her head as she waited for her reply.

"My mother, I did as you instructed me to do. From infancy you have taught me to love the Lord God with all my heart and with all my soul, and I have followed your instructions all of my life. I thank you for your love, for your guidance, for the wonderful Christian example you have shown me." Aquilina stopped momentarily. It was difficult for her to speak now and she tried to find strength to continue. Tears streamed down the cheeks of mother and daughter as they embraced for the last time. "I kept the faith, my mother," she continued, her voice barely a whisper. "I am now returning to the Lord."

With these final words of faith and love, Aquilina committed her pure soul into the Lord's hands. For some time after the last breath left the young girl's body, Aquilina's mother continued to hold her child. Her sorrow was overwhelming but not consuming, for she knew that her child was victorious and had won the crown of glory. She wept the tears only a mother can know, but at the same time thanked God for His great gift. He had not only given her a beautiful, loving, sweet child but a child who was now standing among the Righteous of God.

Later, as the solemn funeral procession wound its way through the town, Aquilina's sacred relics emitted a beautiful fragrance that permeated the atmosphere. A heavenly light was also seen in the night sky that illuminated the saint's tomb and the Christians who witnessed this great sign praised God for accepting one of their own people into His Kingdom.

Saint Celsius

(with Saints Nazarios, Protasios and Gervasios)

October 14

he martyrdom of Saint Celsius is interwoven with the life of Saint Nazarios who lived in Rome in the year 57 A.D. during the reign of the diabolical Emperor Nero. Nazarios, whose parents had been baptized by the Apostle Peter, was a pious child who grew to love God so dearly that, as the years passed, he desired with all his heart to devote himself to the Lord. Giving his material possessions to the poor, he traveled from city to city, winning souls for Christ and baptizing them in the faith. He also distributed alms and ministered to those Christians who had been imprisoned for their devotion to the Lord. In fact, it was in the prison at Milan where Nazarios met the Christian brothers Protasios and Gervasios and spent much time with them encouraging them in their suffering.

One night in a dream, he saw his mother who had a message for him. "Nazarios, my son, I have watched you pursue the path of the Lord God. It is time now for you to travel to Gaul to guide the souls there to the Lord."

Nazarios set off at once, as his mother had instructed, and spread the teachings of Christ to many. Among those whom he led to Christ was a prominent woman of the area who approached him and, handing Nazarios her three-year-old son Celsius, begged him to accept the small boy as his student so that he too might be filled with heavenly joy. The teacher happily accepted the toddler and baptized him.

As the two traveled together throughout Gaul, Nazarios taught with such wisdom and love that his fame became known throughout the region and reached the ears of the ruler Dinovaos who summoned Nazarios and his young disciple to appear before him. Nazarios boldly declared before the ruler that he was a Christian and fearlessly denounced as demons the pagan gods that Dinovaos worshipped. Upon hearing these words, the ruler became furious and, grabbing Celsius from the arms of his teacher, beat him mercilessly.

The toddler did not cower as the ruler had expected. Instead, he spoke up with the innocence only the young possess and said, "My God is the most righteous Judge of all. I love Him very much. He will judge you for all the bad things you do, you wicked man!"

The young child with his teacher was thrown into prison to await a second trial and whatever torments the evil Dinovaos could devise. But when the wife of the ruler saw the handsome young child held as a hostage, she pitied him and begged her husband to release him and his teacher. After some time, Nazarios and Celsius were finally set free.

Once again, the two set out, more determined than ever to spread the teachings of their Lord, Jesus Christ. Instead of proceeding cautiously, fearing further punishment, however, they all the more zealously continued their work and turned more pagans away from the lifeless idols and towards the true faith of Christ.

In the meantime, the hateful Dinovaos sent a letter to Nero informing him of Nazarios' actions as a Christian. Nero immediately summoned the two before him and tried all kinds of devious schemes to lure them away from Christ. But his words had no effect upon the God-fearing servants of the Lord. He tried flattery and threats and promises of wealth, thinking that at least the boy would be won over to the idolaters.

"Young man," Nero warned, looking down upon the small boy standing fearlessly before him. "I am giving you a chance to save yourself. Forget this Jesus your deluded teacher has been telling you about and embrace the mighty gods of Rome. I will shower you with gold and precious jewels. I will give you the best that Rome has to offer. All you have to do is denounce the Nazarene!" Nero grew more upset as the child stood calmly

before him, unimpressed by the imperial treasures. "I command you—bow down before the gods of Rome, you impudent one. I am your emperor! Do as I say!"

The boy would not budge. "I will serve the Lord, Jesus Christ. He is my only ruler," he responded, exhibiting no sign of fear.

Nero was enraged. "Throw both of them into the sea!" he screamed to his men.

The command was carried out at once. To the amazement of all, though, the two servants of God did not drown. An angel of the Lord came to their aid and they walked upon the water to freedom. Seeing this miracle, many witnessing the event embraced the Christian faith.

Freed from Nero by the grace of God, Nazarios and Celsius set out for Genoa, Italy, and then on to Milan to continue preaching the word of God. Once again, they were seized and, at the command of Anulios, were again thrown into prison. Nazarios was joyous, however, for in the prison he was reunited with his friends Protasios and Gervasios. As the friends spoke among themselves about Christ and His teachings, the gloomy, dark dungeon became a fragrant and beautiful paradise where the four loving servants of Christ prayed and joyfully glorified God. Realizing that their earthly days were about to end, the three men prepared young Celsius for the torments that most assuredly lay ahead.

"Celsius, our young friend and co-worker in Christ," Nazarios began, speaking also for the other two Christians, "You have traveled with me and taught with me. Together we have traveled the road leading to the Lord. We four are nearing the end of that road now. But before we can embrace our beloved Jesus, we must endure one last struggle. It will be the most difficult struggle yet. We will suffer greatly and most probably will be killed. Do not think of the pain that we will face. Think what lies ahead for all of us. If we endure to the

end, we will join our beloved Christ in the heavenly man-
sions He has prepared for those who serve Him and love
Him. We have given our lives to Him here on earth in
order that we might live with Him there." Although
Nazarios' words were directed to Celsius, Protasios and
Gervasios derived great comfort from them also.

"Don't worry, my dear teacher and spiritual father, I
am not afraid. You have taught me well. I will never deny
our Christ, for I love Him and long to be with Him forever."

As young Celsius spoke these words, Nazarios knew
that he would be strong. He had shown his courage
before and would exhibit it again.

"Come, my beloved friends," he said, turning to
Protasios and Gervasios. "Let us glorify our great God
together one last time." With Celsius beside him, Nazarios led the group in prayer.

Nero soon learned that Nazarios and Celsius were still
alive, and he was enraged! He immediately sent a fiery
letter to the Genoan ruler, demanding that the prisoners
be beheaded at once and thrown to the wild beasts to be
devoured.

The order was immediately carried out. As the devout
servants of God were led to the place of execution, the
pious Christians who had gathered to pray for them and
to witness their martyrdom were ordered to disperse. The
ruler wanted no one to collect and honor their sacred
remains.

The boy Celsius followed along and bravely waited
his turn to offer his life for his Lord and Savior. His body
had been freed from the dungeon; now his soul would
also be free to soar to the heavenly home that Christ had
prepared for His devoted child.

A few days after their martyrdom, the saints appeared
in a dream to a God-fearing man, instructing him to bury
their bodies and guiding him to the spot where they had

been thrown to the beasts. The faithful Christian did as he was told, collected the holy relics, and took them to his house. As the holy remains of the saints crossed his threshold, the man's daughter, who was a paralytic, was immediately healed, to the joy and amazement of the household.

The sacred bodies were buried in his garden where they remained hidden until the reign of Theodosios the Great in the fourth century. By this time, St. Ambrose had become bishop. Through divine revelation, the pious hierarch discovered the remains of the saints and had them transferred with great reverence and dignity to Milan. As the sacred relics followed the route to their new resting place, many of the ill and afflicted along the way who humbly paid homage to the saints were healed. A great church was built in their honor, and to this day the faithful make pilgrimages there to glorify God Who sends His pious servants to lead us back into His fold.

Saint John of Monembasia

October 24

I n 1758 in the village of Geraki in the southern Greek province of Monembasia, a son
was born to a devout Christian couple. His
father was a priest in the village who, with his
wife, instilled in the child the Orthodox Christian faith
and the lessons of the Holy Scriptures. Young John was
a good and pious lad and increased in wisdom and the
love of God.

But the family's peaceful life was abruptly interrupted
in 1770 when Albanian Moslems, at the command of the
sultan, marched through the Peloponnese Peninsula raid-
ing villages, burning houses and killing some Christians
while enslaving others. The village of Geraki was not to
be spared.

John's beloved father was rounded up with other leaders of the village and brutally slaughtered. The boy and
his mother were among the enslaved and were bought by
a Moslem from Thessaloniki. Though slaves, the two
were together.

Their new Moslem owners were a childless couple
who, upon seeing the handsome, polite and grace-filled
child, desired to adopt him as their own son. Only one
obstacle existed—John had to denounce his Christian
faith and accept Islam. Considering this a simple matter,
the two confronted John who emphatically refused to
deny his Lord and Savior, Jesus Christ. The couple tried
many ways to win the child over, but their promises of
flattery, wealth and glory could not turn his devoted heart
away from his Lord. Day after day both compliments and
threats were presented in hopes of wearing down the
boy's resolve. But John would not yield. He had been

born an Orthodox Christian and would die an Orthodox Christian.

Becoming impatient and angry with John's persistent refusal to obey, the owner began abusing the lad both verbally and physically. He once even pushed him furiously through the street with his sword and turned him over to other Moslems who took turns trying to change his mind with violence. Neither being beaten, nor kicked, nor struck with swords, nor threatened at gun point could frighten him into submission. For two years John and his mother remained servants of this now hateful and vile couple; but as the boy grew, the more his faith and love for Christ increased.

Months passed; and as the summer progressed, the holy feast of the Dormition of the Theotokos, the Mother of God, drew near. The first fourteen days of the month leading up to the holy day on the fifteenth of August were a time of strict fasting and prayer. John, as a good and devout Orthodox Christian, kept the fast despite his circumstances.

When the slave owner realized that John was not eating, he questioned him about the matter. "Why aren't you eating the food I have given you? Isn't it good enough for you? You are a slave and should be glad I even bother to feed you at all!"

At first John said nothing, but as the man continued pressuring him for an answer, he boldly spoke up. "I am an Orthodox Christian and I observe the teachings of my faith. This is a holy time for us and certain foods are forbidden. I will not eat anything my faith prohibits," he firmly stated.

The slave master was furious. "So, you still insist on being a Christian, do you? You refuse to eat my food! Then perhaps you would like to know how starvation feels, young man. After a few days, you will be begging me to feed you and you will eat anything I give you!"

John would not yield to the temptation. Often he was not fed for two or three days in a row. Along with the frequent periods of starvation, the pious youth was harshly tormented. He was beaten, cut with knives, suspended upside down and burned, yet he endured these violent acts patiently and without complaint. Only prayers proceeded from his pure lips.

"My Lord and my God, I love you with all my heart. Be with me; give me strength to endure until my last breath." Such were the words that he quietly uttered over and over again—simple words, but words that greatly empowered him.

John's mother watched as her son slowly wasted away before her very eyes. His body was becoming emaciated, and she found his suffering difficult to bear.

"Eat, my child. Eat enough to stay alive. God understands and will not judge you for eating forbidden foods during the fast. These are exceptional circumstances. Please, John, eat—for my sake. You are my beloved son and I can't bear to see you dying before my eyes. Please, my son, just eat a little food." She tried every way possible to urge the boy to eat, but all efforts to convince him were futile.

"My mother, I know you mean well and are concerned about me. I love you and have always tried to obey you, but I love God more. Fasting is very important for the soul—especially for the soul engaged in spiritual warfare. Many temptations are lurking about me and I need the strength found in prayer and fasting, for prayer and fasting support each other and become stronger. Don't you remember the story of Abraham, who loved and obeyed God so much that he was willing to sacrifice his own son for Him? Have you forgotten, my mother? You must be willing to sacrifice your son also for the sake of the Kingdom of Heaven. I am a priest's son. It is my responsibility to set a good example to others and to practice the faith that you and my father have taught me since birth. You should expect nothing less from me. So, please, my dear mother, do not pressure me to eat as our slave owners do. Instead, pray for me."

A few days later the brutal slave-owner returned, this time threatening the youth with even greater violence if he did not yield to his demands and become a Moslem.

He was determined to use any necessary means to make him obey. Once more, John emphatically refused! In a rage, the wild man stabbed him in the chest and within two days the loving, obedient child of Christ delivered his pure soul into His hands.

At the boy's request, his mother took his precious relics back to his village where they are venerated by pious Christians to this day. On October 24th, the holy Orthodox Church remembers Saint John, the beloved son of Monembasia, the beloved child of God.

Saints Sarbelos, Nita, Hierakos, Theodoulos, Fotios, Vele and Evniki

(with Saints Terentios and Neonilla)

October 28

Terentios and Neonilla were a devout Christian couple who were blessed with seven children whom they raised according to the teachings of Christ. Living during a time of persecution, the family worshipped God secretly yet sincerely.

It was not long, however, before the ruler of the area discovered that they were Christians and commanded that all nine be brought before him for interrogation at once. When ordered to deny Christ, the parents and the children—from the oldest to the youngest—remained loyal to their convictions. Even threats of violent torture could not win them over to the pagans.

For openly confessing their faith, the family was subjected to harsh torments. Their flesh was torn, and vinegar was poured upon the wounds to cause even more suffering. Enduring these afflictions and the fire that followed, the family was led in prayer by their beloved father.

"O Heavenly Father, our only source of comfort and hope, be with us now as we call upon You in our suffering. Keep us strong that we will never deny You. As You have kept us together in this life, keep us together in Your holy kingdom where our sorrow will turn to joy."

As the family prayed, the Lord sent His angels to comfort them and to heal their wounds. When the executioners witnessed this miracle, they were both amazed and terrified. Nevertheless, the wonder did not instill in them any compassion at all, for the family was then thrown into prison and beaten mercilessly. Yet, by the grace of God, they endured whatever affliction the tyrant could conjure—wheels of torture, wild beasts, burning pitch—

but nothing seemed to work upon the pious servants of God, and they remained unharmed through it all.

Finally, when the most brutal torments had failed, Terentios, Neonilla and their children, Sarbelos, Nita, Hierakos, Theodoulos, Fotios, Vele and Evniki, were beheaded. The family that had loved God so dearly that they willingly gave their lives for Him entered the ranks of the holy martyrs together. Both in this world and in the next, they remain a shining example to Christian families throughout the ages.

Saints Asterios, Claudius, Neonos and Neonilla

October 30

Asterios, Claudius and Neonos were brothers who, with their sister Neonilla, lived during the reign of the cruel Emperor Diocletian about the year 288 A.D. After the death of their beloved mother, the children's father remarried; and then, while his children were still young, the father died, leaving them in the care of their greedy stepmother.

With the death of both parents, the children were left with a sizeable inheritance that their stepmother longed to keep for herself. In fact, she desired their wealth so much that she left no stone unturned to obtain it. Finally, she devised a simple yet effective plan. Knowing that the children were devout Christians, she reported them to Lysias, the governor of the region. This action insured her their inheritance, for it was a time of religious persecution and the blood of Christians flowed through the empire.

The children boldly stood before the governor and emphatically presented their case. "O governor, our stepmother is not concerned that we are Christians. She has known this for some time now. Our faith now suits her greedy purpose, however, and she is using it as a means of obtaining the inheritance left to us by our beloved father and mother—an inheritance that is rightfully ours."

Lysias listened to the children, but the possibility of getting his hands on their great fortune appealed to him also. Although he was aware of their stepmother's greedy intentions, he nevertheless favored her side. This was also a welcome opportunity for him to force the siblings to denounce their Christian faith.

"I have listened to your story carefully," Lysias nodded, "and I am willing to strike a bargain with you. If you deny Christ, the treasure will be yours."

The children did not hesitate for a minute in responding to the governor's offer. "We have spoken the truth here today, O Lysias. If you were an honorable man, you would give us what is lawfully ours. Although our parents left us this inheritance, we willingly surrender it to our stepmother, to you, or to anyone else who wants it, for we are not willing to betray our Lord for 'thirty pieces of silver.' Material gains belong to the earthly realm and do not last. We gladly surrender our temporal, earthly treasure for the everlasting treasure that awaits us in God's Kingdom. We will never deny our Christ."

Lysias was enraged! Although the children's inheritance would now be his, his victory was bittersweet. To make it complete would require them to renounce Christ. His attempts at winning them over, he realized, were useless, for he could see in their young faces a great conviction and strength of faith which could not be broken. He had seen such looks too many times in the faces of too many devout Christians who had stood before him in the past—steadfast lovers of Christ who would rather die than renounce their Lord. He paused momentarily to think through this new dilemma. He was Lysias the governor; these were four children. How could he let them defeat him? Perhaps a little physical force would convince them, he thought.

One by one the three brothers were brought before Lysias. One by one they were burned, flogged and ripped to shreds. They were tortured relentlessly until their young bodies looked like one massive wound, yet they would still not renounce their sweetest Lord. Thrown into prison, the boys awaited further torments if they continued to refuse the ruler's demands.

Next, Neonilla, their sister, was brought forward. Lysias was soon to discover that she too shared her brothers' rock of faith and that no torture, no threat of disfigurement would make her forsake Christ. Beaten, burned, hung by her hair, the young girl endured everything, loving her God more than she did her own life. After shearing her head to put her to shame, she was finally burned with fiery coals and surrendered her soul into the hands of her Lord and Savior. Her tattered body was placed in a sack and thrown into the sea.

Asterios, Claudius and Neonos were led outside the walls of the city where they were beheaded. Their pure bodies were left as food for the vultures and wild beasts. Despite the executioner's final cruel acts upon their sacred bodies, the souls of the four young martyrs were at last free to soar to the Heavenly Realm where they enjoy eternal bliss and will stand forever among the Righteous of God.

Saint Plato the Great Martyr

ear Galatia of Asia Minor in the town of Angyra towards the end of the third century lived two pious brothers who loved one another dearly, despite their great age difference. Antiochos,* the elder brother, was a physician who, while healing the bodies of his patients, healed their souls as well with words of righteousness and salvation. Even though Plato was the younger of the two, he was the one who had introduced Antiochos to the Christian faith. Each struggled in his own way to attain the Kingdom of Heaven.

It was a time of harsh persecution and the ruthless Diocletian was the emperor of Rome. But young Plato was not afraid. So greatly did he love the Lord that he zealously pursued every opportunity possible to teach the Christian faith.

As news of his actions spread, Agrippinus, the ruler of the area, lost no time in having the young man arrested and tortured. Thrown into prison, he was brutally beaten by the depraved soldiers who showed no mercy and who taunted him and cursed at him viciously before all who witnessed the torments.

Despite the agony he suffered, young Plato prayed: "My Lord and my God, I put my trust in You. Strengthen me in my struggle. Stand beside me. Do not let me ever deny You, my Christ, for to deny You would be the worst torment of all for my unworthy soul. I do not care for this wretched body. No matter what they may do to it, it is dust. My soul is Yours and Yours alone. Keep it safe, O Lord, that it may return spotless and unstained to Your eternal kingdom."

---

*Antiochos was also canonized by the Church and is commemorated on July 16th.

Agrippinus had ordered the tortures of countless Christians. Torturing the Christians meant two things to the God-hating Agrippinus. First, it was one less Christian to spread the faith, and second, the tortures served as a warning to the multitudes what the followers of Christ could expect if caught. Sadistically enjoying the public "spectacle," Agrippinus had more in store for young Plato. Although the boy's body was already cov-

ered with wounds as he lay in a heap upon the ground, he was then violently stretched upon a bed of fire, all the while enduring further beatings as well. Witnesses to the martyrdom wept openly for the youth and prayed silently that he would stand firm unto death. A number of them, enlightened by the Lord, were inspired by his courage and embraced the Christian faith.

Plato, in excruciating pain, never once uttered a harsh word against his tormentors; neither did he complain. His pure lips only moved in prayer, even as the soldiers pierced him with fiery pellets under his arms and on his sides. The more patience and courage he showed and the more he prayed, the more he was tormented. Hours passed and the young Christian athlete continued the race. The "prize" was the Kingdom of God—a prize well worth the fight. Though his youthful body was beyond recognition, his soul remained firm and fixed upon Christ.

His endurance amazed not only the crowd but also the executioners who, by now, had grown weary themselves. Finally, the order for beheading was given. The young martyr surrendered his soul into the embrace of his Lord. He had won the race; he had attained the holy crown of victory. For his great struggle and endurance, the Church honors him as a "Great Martyr" and celebrates his victory each year on the eighteenth of November.

The Holy Child

(with Saint Romanos)

November 18

ithin the story of the martyrdom of Saint Romanos is found another martyr—a tiny child whose name is known only to God. It happened during the reign of the Roman Emperor Maximian toward the very end of the third century, when a devout man named Romanos lived. A deacon of the church at Caesarea, he was a devout Christian who openly and courageously defended the faith, despite the fact that edicts for the persecution of Christians had been issued.

One day as Asklipiadis, the eparch of the region, was about to enter a pagan temple, Romanos boldly stepped forward and confronted him. "O, eparch Asklipiadis, how can you, a man of great position, enter these pagan temples and waste your time worshiping false idols? You should spend your valuable time instead trying to save your wretched soul. These idols cannot help you in this regard. There is only one true God—the God that we Christians worship—and He is the only one Who can help you. Shouldn't you spend your time on something that is truly beneficial to your soul rather than waste it on false deities? These words of mine are so overwhelmingly sensible and proper and so easy to understand that even a young child can realize the truth in them. A mere infant can tell you that the one God is far superior to your worthless idols!"

"So, you think that I am a fool, do you? Well, we shall see who the fool is here!" snapped Asklipiadis, greatly startled and annoyed by Romanos' outburst. "It is quite easy to dispute your ignorant statement!" He turned and studied the crowd that had gathered, and as he did so, his eye caught sight of a young woman holding a small boy in her arms.

"Bring that child to me!" the eparch ordered. He was certain that he would not only disprove Romanos' statement but would also succeed in humiliating him. The thought made him smile slyly.

Within seconds the guards whisked the small boy away from his mother and presented him to the ruler. The five-year-old who looked up at Asklipiadis, however, was calm and showed no signs of fear.

"My, what a fine young fellow," Asklipiadis said, playing to the crowd. "You seem to be a bright young lad. Now, tell me, should we worship many gods as the Romans do or only one God as the foolish Christians do? Which should we worship?"

The little boy did not hesitate for a minute. Smiling sweetly and innocently, he spoke out loudly enough for all to hear. "The God of the Christians!"

Infuriated and embarrassed, Asklipiadis roughly slapped the child across the face. His fury, however, did not end there. For insulting the ruler and for daring to profess the Christian faith, Romanos' tongue was cut out and he was thrown into prison where even harsher tortures awaited him.

Miraculously, however, the deacon continued to defy the tyrant; for, despite the fact that his tongue had been severed, by God's grace he continued to speak and to glorify Christ. Angering Asklipiadis even more, Romanos was severely tortured and put to death, receiving the crown of martyrdom.

The soldiers then began beating the baby ruthlessly. As he bravely endured his torments, he became thirsty. "May I have some water, please?" he whispered, exerting himself to speak.

"Be patient, my child," his mother answered, stroking his head tenderly. "Do not drink this perishable and lifeless water that the idolaters have; wait until you can drink the living and eternal water of blessedness which our Jesus will give you in His Kingdom," she added tearfully.

Finally, the command of death by beheading was issued. Ever the sweet and loving child of God, the tiny boy left his earthly bonds behind him and entered into the embrace of the Lord. Though his name remains unknown among men, it will be inscribed among the pure and righteous forever.

Saint Philothea the Romanian

December 7

Philothea, a Romano-Bulgarian by birth, was born in the city of Trnovo to a farmer and a Wallachian housewife in 1206. The young girl dearly loved her mother, from whom she had learned the Christian precepts, and her devotion to the Lord and His commandments increased. But her peaceful, happy home life would not last long, because when Philothea was still quite young, her beloved mother died.

In time her father remarried, leaving his daughter in the care of his new wife who sought every opportunity to punish the child and belittle her in the eyes of her father.

"Your daughter, that Philothea," she complained to her husband, "can never do anything right. She doesn't obey me; she's lazy; she will never amount to anything!" she nagged, making up more lies about the girl with each passing minute. "All she wants to do is go to church—as if that will help her at all! And those children she insists on feeding—those little wretches. She takes our good food and gives it to those orphans on the street. Something must be done about her, and soon!"

"Yes, you are right, something should be done," the girl's father agreed. "Philothea!" he shouted, "come here at once!"

The young girl ran into the room as quickly as she could. She tried everything possible to keep from angering the couple but they always found something to scold her about anyway.

"Yes, my father, what do you want?" the child asked softly.

"Your mother here tells me that you are disobedient. She also informs me that you spend far too much time in church and that you give our hard-earned food to those poor oafs in the neighborhood. I command you to stop this foolishness at once! Do you understand?"

"Yes, my father," the girl replied, "I will try to do as you say."

Philothea showed tremendous patience and courage. Though only twelve years old, she possessed a great maturity and spiritual strength and determined to continue the Christian virtues she had learned while sitting in her own mother's lap. She prayed, fasted, distributed food and clothing to the poor, and lived a pure and holy life, despite the difficult circumstances that prevailed in her home.

As autumn approached, Philothea's father spent long days in the fields harvesting his crops. It was Philothea's duty to take him food as he worked. But each day as she set out, the compassionate child took a small portion from her father's overly abundant meal and offered it to the poor children she met along the way. When her father realized that his plate seemed to be missing a small amount of food each day, he confronted his wife.

"Why are you putting less food in my plate? Don't you know how hard I work and how hungry I get working out in the fields? Is it too much for a man to expect a complete meal?" he yelled.

"Why don't you ask Philothea what happened to it? I told you she doesn't listen to either of us. She does as she pleases around here and gets away with it. She has probably distributed it to those filthy orphans again!" she hissed.

The next day the father decided to follow Philothea in order to catch her in the act of distributing his food to the needy. As the young girl appeared and moved among the less fortunate, her father, overcome with rage, threw a hatchet at the child, hitting her in the leg. The injury proved to be fatal as the girl bled profusely. She died in the streets among the poor whom she so greatly loved and entered the Kingdom of the Righteous.

The father, with great remorse and fear, immediately realized his great sin. He ran to Philothea, attempting to lift her body from the ground, but was unable to do so as her weight had become very great. Filled with guilt, he presented himself before the Archbishop of Trnovo to confess his great crime against his daughter.

With candles and incense, the clergy of the town followed the archbishop in procession to the girl's body, but even their attempts at lifting her proved unsuccessful. Realizing that a greater force was at work, the archbishop prayed for guidance to discern the wishes of God for His young servant. He was perplexed where to place her remains if they would be able to lift them. The names of many churches and monasteries were mentioned, but still the sacred body would not be moved. When, at last, the Monastery of Curtea de Arges was named, the relics became as light as a feather and were immediately placed into a coffin. In the procession, the relics were taken as far as the Danube River where Romanian clergy, monastics and laymen escorted the saint to Curtea de Arges Monastery for burial.

Each year on December seventh, the feast day of the young martyr, Saint Philothea is visited and honored by pilgrims who venerate her remains and beseech her with prayers for the sick. Many of the faithful have been healed and many other miracles have occurred through her intercessions. In times of drought the saint continues to this day to show her love and compassion. When the sacred relics are escorted in procession through the arid fields by the faithful, miracles still occur. Through her prayers, God sends the much-needed rains and blesses the farmlands for yet another season.

Backing her faith with "works," Philothea lived the true Christian principles taught by the Lord. Her unselfish love and compassion for those less fortunate earned her a place before the throne of God where she intercedes on behalf of all who approach her in faith.

Saint John of Thasos

t was the year 1652 during the Turkish Occupation of the eastern lands that a pious young lad lived in the sparsely inhabited town of Maries on the Greek island of Thasos. Little is known of his life except that, at the age of fourteen, he was sent to the bustling city of Constantinople to learn the trade of a tailor. A certain Christian accepted him as an apprentice and began teaching him all he needed to succeed in his chosen field.

One day his master sent him to a Jewish merchant to purchase threads. Seeing his youth, the man attempted to cheat him in the transaction, but when John confronted him, a dispute erupted. To get even with the lad, the merchant took advantage of the Moslem hour of prayer. When the muezzin ascended the minaret to call his people to worship, the shopkeeper opened the door and screamed loudly, "John has mocked your faith; he has slandered Islam!"

John was shocked! He was quiet and respectful and would have never spoken these words. He was also very bright and knew that such comments would easily arouse the wrath of the Moslems.

Several Turks immediately seized the lad and began beating him violently. They accused him before the vizier who, noting his youth and how decently and logically he spoke, tried to lure him into the Moslem ranks.

"Let me help you, young man," he began, falsely assuming an air of concern. "You are a Christian; we are Moslems. We are your masters, however. Isn't it logical then for you to comply with our wishes and join our ranks? If you confess our faith, you will receive great riches and position. You will never be in need of anything again."

His words were wasted on the noble John. "You are not my masters and never will be," he replied. "My only Master is the Lord, Jesus Christ, and Him only will I serve. I will never leave my Christian faith for Islam. I will never deny my Christ! You are foolish to expect me to ever do such a thing! Neither am I intrigued by your offers of wealth and position. The material things with which you try to impress me are nothing to me. I am committed to Christ, my Lord and Savior, and nothing you can say or do to me will ever change my conviction and my love for Him."

When the defeated Turks saw that John could not be swayed, they sentenced the innocent boy to death. Led "as a sheep to the slaughter," the pious boy knelt before his executioner. He made the sign of the cross and, after asking God to be with him, he bent his neck to await the blow that would end his short life.

The evil executioner, annoyed by John's sincere faith and devotion to Jesus Christ, decided to make his suffering more grievous by using slow, short strokes. The young Christian, however, endured patiently without uttering any cries of fear or pain. Instead, he anxiously awaited his martyric end with joy. Finally, the executioner gave the final blow, freeing John's pure soul to enter the realm of the righteous.

During the night, devout Christians carried his sacred remains to the cemetery at Begoglou, a place forever blessed by his holy presence.

Saint Evodos and his Brothers

(with Saint Theodote)

December 22

Theodote was a pious Christian woman from Nicaea of Bithynia who raised her three sons according to the teachings of Christ. Hearing of the good works of Saint Anastasia, the Deliverer from Potions, Theodote had often considered joining her in her mission.

Levkadios, the idolatrous ruler, however, knew about Theodote, and at the prompting of the depraved Emperor Diocletian he considered marrying her. The devious emperor had hoped that by Levkadios' marriage with the young widow, Levkadios would be able to force Theodote away from her Christian faith.

"Diocletian is right," Levkadios thought to himself. "Theodote is quite a remarkable woman. She is lovely and good. I shall ask her this very day to become my wife."

Levkadios found Theodote at once and asked for her hand in marriage. He anxiously awaited her reply.

"Levkadios, your offer is most kind and generous, but it is so sudden." Theodote was cautious. She had no intention of marrying Levkadios, but at the same time, she did not want to anger him. She knew of his friendship with the wicked Diocletian and was concerned for the safety of her young children. "I have three sons to take care of. Therefore, please give me some time to think this over. After all, marriage is a very serious decision."

"Of course, my dear," Levkadios answered. "I understand. This proposal is rather sudden. Just don't take too much time to make your decision."

As soon as Levkadios left, Theodote knew she had to move quickly. She immediately called her sons together, collected a few personal belongings and fled from Nicaea. This was the opportune time for the family to find Anastasia and become a part of her mission.

As time passed and Levkadios heard nothing from Theodote, his intended bride, he decided to stop by her house himself. Upon his arrival, however, he was shocked to discover that she and her sons had left. With a wounded ego, he frantically searched the region to find her. When at last he learned that she had joined the small

group of Christians, Levkadios was furious. At his command, Theodote and her three boys were bound and sent to the ruler of Bithynia who tried every possible way to convince them to embrace the pagan idols. His efforts failed, for Theodote and her sons remained steadfast in their love for Christ.

The ruler had a devious plan. "I have heard that this Theodote is a strong-willed Christian. Let's see just how stubborn she will remain if she watches her children suffer! I'm certain she will give in to my demands after we present her with that threat."

The ruler looked at the young family standing before him. "Guards! Bring the oldest boy to me at once!" he demanded sharply.

Young Evodos walked fearlessly toward the ruler and looked him in the eye.

"Are you ready to denounce this Christ whom you and your family serve?'

"Never, O ruler," Evodos boldly replied.

"You realize what will happen to you and your brothers if you refuse my offer, don't you? And it will not go well for your mother either. I warn you, young man. Think carefully before giving me your answer!"

"My answer is ready," the lad responded. "I will never deny my Christ. You are the one who needs to think carefully, for your soul will suffer greatly if you continue worshiping these false deities of yours."

"You have a sharp tongue for such a young fellow. Is this how your mother has raised you?" the ruler asked sarcastically.

"My mother is a good mother and has taught my brothers and me the truth. She has filled our lives with the most valuable gifts—gifts that are good for our souls. She has not instilled within us the desire for material things that do not last but, instead, has prepared us for salvation that will be eternal. She has taught us to love

Christ, the only God. He is the only one we will serve. His Kingdom is our goal. Your threats don't frighten us. Do whatever you want. We will never deny our God."

For his sincere devotion to Christ, Evodos was harshly beaten before the eyes of his mother, who encouraged her son to face martyrdom, just as she had encouraged other devout Christians whom she had visited in the prisons.

Unsuccessful in his attempts to win the family over to the pagan side, the tyrant ordered that Theodote and her children be thrown into a fiery furnace. Evodos, his brothers, and his mother joyfully and courageously faced death and together received the sacred crowns of martyrdom. A church was built in honor of the holy martyrs at Kambos.

The Holy Infants of Bethlehem

December 29

> "A voice was heard in Ramah,
> Lamentation and bitter weeping,
> Rachel weeping for her children
> Refusing to be comforted...
> Because they are no more."
> Jeremiah 31:15

This prophecy of Jeremiah, centuries before the coming of the Messiah, was fulfilled approximately a year after the birth of Jesus and is related in the first chapter of the Gospel of Saint Matthew.

While Saint Stephen and Saint Thekla have the unique distinction of being the first male and female who willingly gave their lives for Christ, years earlier, fourteen thousand innocent babies became the very first children to die for the Lord. Snatched from the arms of their horrified parents, they were brutally slaughtered by a demonic King Herod who feared the newborn Christ Child so much that he ordered the deaths of the most innocent beings of all.

When Jesus was born, Magi from the East saw an unusual star in the heavens, and they followed its light, perceiving that it foretold the birth of a new king. Before reaching their destination, though, they stopped at Jerusalem at the palace of King Herod. After the preliminary introductions, they came to the real reason for their visit.

"We have been following an unusual star in the heavens, your Majesty, and perceive that it heralds the birth of a new king. Most assuredly you, as king, will be able to direct us to this newborn child."

But Herod knew nothing about the birth of a new king. The very thought of it terrified him, since he wanted no new rivals to his throne.

"It seems that perhaps I have heard of some such prophecy," he lied. "If you will allow me a little time, I will find out further details for you."

As the Magi rested from their long journey, Herod frantically called his chief priests and scribes to find

some answers to this new dilemma. After poring through the ancient texts, they reported back to the ruler.

"Your Highness, it seems that a prophecy of a Messiah does indeed exist. He is to be born in Judea in the town of Bethlehem."

King Herod was greatly distressed by this news. His face paled at the thought of a rival to his throne. "I must destroy this baby before he threatens my crown," he quietly plotted to himself. He slowly paced back and forth for a while to plan his strategy. As he mentally devised his malicious scheme, he summoned the Magi.

"I have news for you," he said, approaching the three men with a devious grin. "The ancient prophecies state very clearly that a Messiah is to be born in Bethlehem of Judea. Quickly go and find him, and then come back to me and tell me where he is so that I can also go and honor him."

The Magi bowed to the ruler and hurried off to Bethlehem to pursue their quest. There, in the city of David, they found more than they had ever anticipated. They expected to find an earthly king; they found instead the Heavenly King, the Christ Child, the Son of God. With great joy and excitement in their hearts, they prepared to return to Herod with the good news.

That night, however, they had a dream. The powerful words they heard in it remained with them. "Do not return to Herod. He has deceived you. He fears the Son of God and wants to destroy Him. Take another route as you return to your homeland." The Magi obeyed their divine dream.

As time passed and the Magi never returned to him with news of the new king, Herod became furious. "How dare they not return to me! I am the king! They're obliged to obey my orders!" he ranted, waving his arms as he stormed through his palace. "I'll find the child myself! I don't need their help!" In a rage, he ordered the slaughter of all male infants two years old and under throughout Bethlehem and its surrounding districts.

His madness did not end there, however. He also had Zachariah, the father of John the Baptist, killed because he would not reveal where his son John could be found. In his anger he even turned on his advisors, the seventy members of the Sanhedrin who informed him of the prophecy of the coming Messiah.

But Herod's violent crimes would not go unpunished. He was struck down with a horrible condition: worms devoured his flesh and the putrid sores spread an unbearable stench. He died an agonizing death and, because of his wickedness, lost his soul as well.

The holy young infants whose deaths helped to protect the newborn Christ are commemorated by the Church on December 29th. Baptized in the blood of martyrdom, they will be remembered always as the first to give their lives for the Son of God.

Saints Pevsippos, Elasippos and Mesippos

(with Saint Neonilla)

January 16

Pevsippos, Elasippos and Mesippos were triplets from Cappadocia who were extremely skillful at riding and taming wild horses. One day a festival was to be held in the region and the boys invited Neonilla, their grandmother, to the celebration.

Neonilla was a devout Christian and, saddened by the fact that her grandsons had been raised as pagans, set out to share her faith with them. The lads were very bright and, like a sponge, absorbed the teachings of Christ into their thirsty young souls. So zealous were they in their newly found faith that they set out proclaiming Christ and, in their fervor, smashed the lifeless, pagan idols. For this they were arrested and thrown into prison.

Upon hearing of their plight, Neonilla visited them and encouraged them. "My dearest grandsons, the beloved sons of my own child, by God's love and mercy, you listened to my words when I spoke to you about Christ. Now you will face the most difficult and most important challenge of your young lives. Wild horses are nothing compared to the great temptations that await you. Tame the fears within you as you once tamed the unruly beasts. As you learned the skill of riding, you will now master the skill of spiritual warfare. I am not worried about you because I know that your love for our Lord is great. He did not call you to Him only to let your souls perish now. Be brave; be strong, my darlings. You have won victories in the past, yet those do not compare to the victory you will attain today if you endure. Winning this contest will secure for you the precious crowns of martyrdom, the prize of eternal life."

One by one, the three boys embraced their loving grandmother whom they adored. She had given them more than her love; she had given them Christ, and His radiant light burned within them.

The boys suffered many torments before they were burned to death. However, the wicked idolaters were not yet finished with the family. Neonilla herself, the pious grandmother, was beheaded and, receiving the crown of a martyr as well, stands with her beloved grandsons in God's Kingdom.

Saint Neofytos

o the pious Christian couple, Theodoros and Florentia, a son was born and given the name Neofytos. It was the end of the third century during the reigns of the Christian-haters, Decius and Diocletian, and persecutions of Christians were rampant.

A devout and reverent child, Neofytos was filled with God's grace since birth—a grace within him that was nurtured in his home and that continued to enlighten his soul. Compassionate and kind from an early age, the boy often prayed to God fervently to give him food to distribute among his poor schoolmates, and the merciful Lord always granted his petition.

Also during these years a dove appeared to him and, perched atop the boy's bed, kept watch over him as he slept. At times the bird also spoke to him. On one such occasion Neofytos' mother immediately died from fright when she overheard the bird speak. But the Lord heard the pure and righteous prayers of young Neofytos for his mother and brought her back to life.

Soon afterwards, Neofytos was led by the Spirit to a cave on Mount Olympus where an angel of the Lord ministered to his needs for two years. It was in this ascetic environment in the care of the Lord that the young boy lived and prayed and grew in spirit. Briefly visiting his home at the age of eleven in order to distribute his material possessions to the poor and to see his parents for the last time, the boy returned to his beloved cave where he continued his ascetic struggles.

Four years later, the young Christian again received a command from an angel of the Lord. "Neofytos, go quickly to the Emperor Decius and confess your belief in Christ."

Upon hearing these words, the young ascetic unquestioningly set out to obey the angel's command. His love for the Lord was great and he was humbled by the opportunity to proclaim this love for Him openly before the emperor.

Standing before Decius, Neofytos boldly and without hesitation spoke out. "I have come here today, O emperor, to publicly declare before you and before all of the citizens of Rome my great devotion and love for my God and Savior Jesus Christ. You have heard of Him, I am

sure, and yet you do not know Him. But I can testify before you that He is indeed the Son of God and I shall honor Him forever."

Decius was enraged at the words of the fifteen-year-old. "How dare you stand before me and profess this Christian faith of yours? Don't you realize who I am? Don't you know that I can kill you on the spot if I so choose? Why, I have killed hundreds of followers of your sect—thousands!" Decius screamed. "Their lives meant nothing to me and neither does yours! Take him away!" he yelled to his soldiers.

For Neofytos' open defiance, Decius had him harshly beaten and then thrown into a fiery oven to be burned alive. Neofytos, however, remained unharmed. Since the fire did not consume him, he was then cast to the wild beasts. Protected by the Lord once again, he emerged safely.

Because the boy had remained untouched despite the violence inflicted upon him, Decius and many of the pagans present were infuriated. Wild with rage, one barbarian in the group drew his sword and lunged at the lad, inflicting a mortal wound.

Neofytos, the child of God, though dead to this temporal world, won eternal life in the Kingdom of Heaven and was adorned with the crown of martyrdom. He died as he had lived—ever obedient to the will of God—even unto death.

Saints Theodoti, Theoktisti and Evdoxia

(with Saints Athanasia, Cyrus and John)

January 31

During the reign of the Emperor Diocletian about the year 292 A.D, there lived two pious Christians—Cyrus from Alexandria, Egypt, and John from Edessa. In order to escape religious persecution, Cyrus fled to a monastery near the Arabian Gulf. Living a strict ascetic life of fasting and prayer, he advanced so much spiritually that God bestowed upon him the gift of healing.

When John, while traveling in Jerusalem, learned of the miracles of the servant of God, Cyrus, he ran to join him in his service. The two devout men worked together, and by God's grace they cured the infirm in body and soul, while spreading the teachings of Christ to all who would listen.

One day the two men received news of Athanasia, a virtuous Christian woman who had been imprisoned for the faith with her three young daughters, Theodoti, fifteen years old, Theoktisti, thirteen, and Evdoxia, eleven. Fearing that the women might deny the faith under persecution, the two men set out for the prison to offer them support and encouragement to face the trials that lay before them.

"Peace be to you," the men said as they approached Athanasia and her three young girls in the prison. "We are Cyrus and John, the unworthy servants of the Lord God Jesus Christ, and we have come here to pray with you in your hour of peril."

"Welcome, my friends," Athanasia smiled. "We welcome your prayers as well. My daughters and I are about to face unknown trials because of our faith in our Christ. We are not afraid, though, for we know that the Lord is with us, for He has sent you, his beloved servants, to us. Though my daughters are young, their love for the Lord is strong. Nothing that the guards can do to us can turn us away from Him. He has always remembered us in this

life and He will continue to care for us in the heavenly life also."

Athanasia was radiant and calm as she spoke. There was no fear in her whatsoever. The two men were equally impressed with the three young sisters who stood before them as well, for despite their tender years, they too were at peace and exhibited not even a hint of fear. They breathed a sigh of relief and silently thanked God for coming to the aid of this young family.

The six devoted Christians quietly prayed together in the confines of the dreary prison. "Our Heavenly Father, we thank You for the blessings which You have always bestowed upon us, Your unworthy servants. We humbly ask You to hold us in Your immaculate hands and to direct our paths according to Your divine will. We are ready to lay down our lives for You."

When the ruler of the district learned that Cyrus and John had come to the aid of Athanasia and her children, he was furious and immediately commanded that the men be tortured. Now it was the women's turn to encourage Cyrus and John.

"O loving Father, our Lord, Jesus Christ, come to the aid of Cyrus and John. They have loved You and are willing to die for You. Give them strength; give them the courage and patience to endure the agonies that await them. Grant that they may feel Your awesome presence, and comfort them in their hour of need."

With the men out of the way, the tyrant turned his attention to Athanasia and her children. Because they were women and also young, the ruler ignorantly expected them to buckle under pressure and to denounce their Lord readily. He was greatly mistaken, however. Little did he realize that the immovable wall of Christian piety stood before him. Despite their youth, Theodoti, Theoktisti and Evdoxia stood fearlessly beside their mother and boldly declared their devotion to Christ even unto death.

Subjected to brutal beatings that deeply tore into their flesh, the three young sisters would not renounce their faith. Along with their beloved mother Athanasia, they were at last beheaded along with Cyrus and John. The six loyal servants of Christ joyfully bent their necks before the executioner and received the holy crowns of martyrdom. The Church remembers their entry into the Kingdom of Heaven on January 31st.

Saint Agathi

In the Sicilian town of Catania during the violent reign of Decius, there lived a God-fearing young virgin named Agathi. Her parents, both idolaters, had died, leaving their daughter free to embrace the Christian faith and to devote her life to Christ, Whom she loved above all. Extremely wealthy, the compassionate young maiden lavishly distributed her personal property among the poor. She possessed many God-given qualities—among them, a rare, exquisite beauty of both body and soul. However, despite her beauty and wealth, Agathi remained unspoiled and sought only heavenly treasures, turning her back on the world's treasures.

News of this exceptional handmaiden of God spread throughout the area and reached Quintianus, the governor of Sicily. Of low birth, he desired to take the fifteen-year-old as his wife in order to raise his own status. Stories of her great physical beauty increased his desire to marry her.

Summoning the girl to appear before him, Quintianus first sought with flattery and compliments to win her affections. "O lovely maiden, I have called you here to see for myself if the things I have heard about you are true. Now that you stand before me, I am convinced of their validity. Such exquisite beauty is rare. Why, it is as if a lovely flower had entered my presence," he continued, casting a sly smile. "You are most fortunate, my dear—perhaps the most fortunate girl around—for I have chosen you to be my wife. You will live a grand life by my side. Palaces and jewels, fine linens and gold, all will be yours soon, my beautiful one." The governor walked about as he spoke, looking at the young girl and anxiously anticipating her affirmative reply. She could never refuse his offer! Soon she would belong to him.

It was Agathi's turn to speak now. The governor's words had repulsed her. "O Governor Quintianus, perhaps many women would be honored to be your wife and would be tremendously flattered that you have chosen them. The thought of gold and jewels and such things would indeed appeal to them. However, I, O governor, am not one of those women. I am not impressed by your offers of gold and fine linens; neither do I seek the finest positions at Rome's lavish feasts. Most of all, I do not wish to become your wife."

Quintianus was stunned! How could anyone refuse such a grand proposal? "Are you crazy?" he asked Agathi, unable to comprehend the reasons for her rejection. "Are you fully aware of my power and rank? If you know what is best for you, you will reconsider my offer while I am still willing to accept you!" he stated arrogantly.

"I have given you my answer," the young girl responded. "I do not wish to become your wife. I have only one bridegroom—my Lord Jesus Christ—and He is the only one I choose to serve. He is my Lord and Master, my Creator and my Father. He is my life and my joy. Apart from Him, nothing has value for me. The hollow things that you offer are man-made symbols of rank and prestige. Only the shallow strive to attain such possessions. They mean nothing to me."

Although his great ego had been bruised, Quintianus was amazed that one so young and lovely could also be so eloquent. She had embarrassed him before his court, but he was not willing to concede his defeat yet.

There lived in the city a woman of ill-repute named Aphrodisia, who plied her filthy trade throughout the region with her nine equally vile daughters. He sent for

the woman and said, "There is something very important
that I want you to do for me. If you are successful, you
will receive unlimited wealth and a life of untold luxury.
There is a young girl—Agathi—whom I wish to take as
my wife. She is beautiful and of noble birth, but unfortunately, she is a follower of the Crucified One. She has
refused my offer of marriage. Imagine that! She has
refused me!" He shook his head in disbelief as he spoke.

"I want you to take her for a month and convince her to change her mind. Introduce her to the ways of the world. Make her accept the gods of Rome. Do this, Aphrodisia, and you will be greatly rewarded."

For a whole month Aphrodisia and her daughters attempted in every possible way to persuade Agathi to share their perverted lifestyle. She tried using threats, force and flattery, but nothing worked, for the righteous Agathi would neither deny Christ nor defile her pure body or soul.

After thirty days, Aphrodisia reported back to Quintianus. The governor could tell by the look on her face that her efforts had failed. "Mighty governor," the woman said, "it would be much easier to bend iron than to bend the will of Agathi!"

The governor was enraged that his plan had failed. He continued provoking and interrogating Agathi, but to no avail. Finally, he resorted to violence. He ordered that she be beaten and thrown into prison without food or water, hoping in this way to weaken her and frighten her into submission. But when she again stood before the ruler the next day, she boldly reaffirmed her commitment to Jesus Christ.

Quintianus finally gave up. He had been defeated and commanded that she be subjected to the most vicious torments imaginable. Every means of torture was used: whips, swords, flaming iron rods, fire. While still bleeding profusely from her mutilation and almost beyond recognition, Agathi was again thrown into the dark prison.

She was not alone there, however. In the middle of the night a magnificent light radiated in the darkness, and in the midst of this divine light stood an elderly man carrying a vessel in his hands. Beside him was a youth holding a large candle. Not knowing who they were, the suffering maiden at first refused their offers of help. She trusted only in the Lord God and knew that, if it were His will, she would be healed. The elderly guest gently said, "Agathi, I am the Apostle Peter and standing beside us is your own guardian angel. We have been sent by God to comfort you and to heal your wounds, dear child."

Agathi was miraculously healed, and the two disappeared as quickly as they had come. The young martyr tearfully fell to her knees, praising God and thanking Him for His great goodness and mercy.

The next day when she was taken to Quintianus, the tyrant was both startled and furious that the young girl was whole again. "Who has dared to come to your aid, you wretched girl?" he screamed. "How did they get past my guards?"

"No earthly power has healed me. I was healed by my Lord and Savior Jesus Christ, Who did not forget about me in the dungeon and Who has been standing beside me throughout my trials," Agathi proclaimed joyously.

The governor flew into a rage. He ordered his men to light a huge fire and to bind the girl with chains and throw her into it. Agathi prayed, as she had throughout her contest. "My dearest Lord and Savior, I, Your unworthy servant seek Your aid once again. Stand beside me as you have since my struggle began and give me the courage and patience to endure. I bend to Your divine will, my Christ, in all things."

Immediately, a violent earthquake shook the city. Countless homes and buildings throughout Catania were destroyed, including the governor's palace, and two of his advisors were killed. The people demanded that Quintianus cease his evil tortures upon the innocent girl because they believed that it was his great sin that had caused the devastation to their city. Fearing the threats of the angry mob, the governor ordered his men to release Agathi and to return her to the prison. To the amazement of all, the holy child was unharmed.

Back in the prison Agathi fell to her knees before the Lord: "O Heavenly Father, I thank You for Your abundant blessings." She was filled with emotion, and tears streamed down her face and collected in a small puddle on the prison floor. Her prayer was interspersed with moments of profound silence during which she paused to feel Christ's healing touch upon her weary soul. "My dearest Jesus," she continued, "thank you for letting me, Your most wretched child, suffer for You. Each stroke of the executioner's whip, each wound upon my flesh has brought me closer to You. You have cleansed me with the baptism of martyrdom that my soul might come before Your holy presence dressed in a white garment. If You so will, my beloved Christ, take my soul into Your Kingdom, and grant that I might see Your holy and glorious countenance." As these tender words emerged from deep within her heart and fell from her most pure lips, Agathi's gentle soul was carried beyond the heavenly gates to behold forever the glory of God.

The Christians of the city reverently prepared her sacred relics for burial and, at the time of her interment, one hundred angels dressed in white suddenly appeared and escorted her holy body with honor to its final resting place. One angel, approaching the tomb, covered it with a marble slab upon which had been written the words: "A mind holy and willing, the honor of God and the deliverance of the fatherland."

Quintianus was punished for his crimes the same day. Upon hearing of Agathi's death, he rushed out to claim her vast properties for himself. While attempting to cross a river, he was thrown from his horse and violently trampled under its feet. His body fell into the water and was never found.

Saint Fausta

(with Saints Evilasios and Maximos)

February 6

In Kyzikos during the reign of the Emperor Maximian in the early fourth century, there lived a beautiful Christian girl named Fausta. Her parents were not only devout but also quite wealthy and, upon their death, left their daughter a great fortune.

Despite her youth and her vast riches, Fausta continued living the Christian virtues that had been instilled in her since birth. She was virtuous and compassionate and devoted her life to prayer, fasting and the study of Sacred Scripture.

When the pious, young girl's fame reached the emperor, Evilasios, a pagan priest, was assigned to question her. He was happy to do so, for he had heard many things about her and wanted very much to see her for himself.

As Fausta drew near, Evilasios was startled by her youth. He had heard of her virtue and compassion, her life of prayer and study and had expected one of more mature years.

"How old are you, child?" he asked.

"I am thirteen years old," she replied.

"I have heard much about you," he continued. "What disturbs me the most, however, is that you are a Christian. Am I right or do you deny this?"

"I will never deny the fact that I am a Christian. I am a Christian and will remain one forever," Fausta vowed.

"Do you know that by admitting you are a Christian, you have just sentenced yourself to extreme torture and possibly even death?" Evilasios added threateningly.

"Yes, I am aware of that also, but my answer is still the same."

"Don't be foolish, young lady," the pagan scoffed. "You have wealth and beauty and fame. Why throw it all away? Worship our gods and save your life! Otherwise, you will be drowned in the sea!"

"The Lord God has given me much, O Evilasios, this is true. How then could I ever turn my back on Him and pursue your false beliefs? I will never leave Him, for He is my Lord and Savior!"

For refusing to deny her Lord and God, Fausta was subjected to harsh torments. Though she suffered greatly, she never once opened her mouth to complain or to protest her cruel treatment.

Evilasios was puzzled as he watched Fausta's endurance under torture. How could one so young and so beautiful also be so courageous? By God's grace, the pagan priest soon came to his senses; he turned from idolatry and embraced the one true God.

News of this conversion spread quickly! Maximian was enraged and immediately sent the eparch, Maximos, to punish both Fausta and the new Christian, Evilasios. Although the severest of tortures were inflicted upon the two, they remained steadfast in the faith and refused to denounce Jesus Christ, the Savior.

When a cauldron of boiling water was prepared to further test the faith of Fausta and Evilasios, Maximos marveled at their courage. He realized at last that their strength came from their continuous prayers to Christ, for he had heard the quiet supplications that had fallen from their lips throughout their ordeal. By God's great mercy and compassion, the eparch also accepted the Christian faith, and for this was thrown into the cauldron to suffer with the other two Christians.

Through her great love and devotion to Christ, Fausta willingly gave her life for the faith and saved the souls of two others as well. Along with her, Evilasios and Maximos also received the sacred crowns of martyrdom and entered into the Kingdom of God where they are numbered among the saints.

Saint Likarion

(with Saints Martha and Mary)

February 6

artha and Mary were sisters who lived with their mother and their young brother Likarion in Asia Minor. The devout family not only lived the Christian ideals but also boldly proclaimed their faith among the pagans of the district.

One day the sisters watched as a military commander and his men marched by their house. Unafraid of the consequences, they ran out to meet him as he passed their door. "Mighty commander, you pass our door with much pageantry and pomp. But your glory is nothing compared to our Master's glory."

"And just who is this master of yours?" he glared at them.

"Our Lord and Master is Christ the Lord, the God of heaven and earth," the two girls professed before the commander who was startled by their boldness.

"Seize them!" he loudly commanded his men, "They are Christians and all such fools must be banished from the face of the earth!"

The two girls were immediately arrested. Their young brother, Likarion, was spotted as he watched the terrifying events unfold before his eyes from the doorway and was taken into custody with his sisters. Mary and Martha, with the young boy, were dragged away and sentenced to death.

When their pious mother learned of their plight, she hastened to their side. Stroking their heads tenderly, she spoke to them softly. "My children, your hour of suffering has approached. I never imagined a day would come when you would be taken from me. My heart is heavy, for you have been my greatest joy. I offer you to the Lord, in Whose hands you have been since birth. This day will soon end as will your suffering, and then you will know the peace that only our Lord can give. Be brave; stand firm in your faith. And know that I will always love you." With this, the courageous mother watched her children as they were taken to their deaths.

Martha and Mary were pierced with spears; Likarion was beheaded. The three loyal servants of God surrendered their pure souls into His hands and received the sacred crowns of martyrdom. Their mother watched as their last breaths left their young bodies. She smiled a knowing smile, despite the tears that flowed down her cheek. Her children were now at peace, as she had promised them; their suffering had ended.

Two Holy Children

(with Saint Vlasios)

February 11

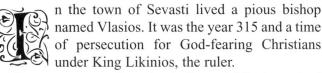n the town of Sevasti lived a pious bishop named Vlasios. It was the year 315 and a time of persecution for God-fearing Christians under King Likinios, the ruler.

After many years of service in Sevasti, Vlasios retired to a mountain cave where he spent his hours in prayer. He was given so much grace that he tamed the wild beasts that approached his shelter. For his spiritual labors and his great piety and virtue, Vlasios was bestowed the gift of healing which he lovingly and compassionately offered to his people. At the same time, he spread the faith and guided many souls to Christ.

Bishop Vlasios' tranquil life was not to last, however. His cave was soon discovered and the pagans dragged him before the governor of Agricola for trial. Refusing to worship the lifeless idols of the pagans, the bishop suffered various tortures at the hands of his captors before being thrown into prison to await further sentencing. Seven devout women followed him into the prison and were beheaded after confessing their Christian beliefs.

It was at this time also that the martyr met two young children who were to be his final students and companions. Their prison cell became a catechetical school as Vlasios spoke to them about Christ.

"Dear children," the kind bishop began, "you have been alone and, I would imagine, very frightened by all the changes in your young lives. Do not fear, for Christ our Lord is with all of us here in this prison. I am glad He has brought us together to face this final trial. Soon we will be with Him; we must only be strong until the end. Pray to Him, and He will hear your petitions, for our Christ always hears the prayers of children." The children listened intently to their new teacher and friend. "We will do as you say, sir. We will be strong, for we love the Lord also. Soon we will be together in His heavenly home."

The old bishop smiled. They were so young, so innocent. He wondered, "Do they really understand what awaits them? Can they endure?" Somehow, he knew that all would be well. With God's help, they would all endure.

When the day of sentencing arrived, Bishop Vlasios was brought forth. He was thrown into a deep lake, but an angel of the Lord delivered him unharmed.

Enraged that his efforts at convincing Vlasios to renounce Christ had been futile, the governor ordered Vlasios and his two young students to be beheaded. Strengthened by their teacher, the children courageously faced death with him. As God had provided for them in the dark confines of the prison by sending them a guardian and friend, likewise he welcomed them together into His Kingdom. The Church remembers them on February 11th.

Saints Mavros and Jason

(with Saints Claudius and Hilaria)

March 19

laudius was a judge during the reign of the Roman Emperor Numerianos who had overseen the persecutions of Saints Chrysanthos and Daria, a devout Christian couple who had been arrested for openly preaching the faith. Marveling at their endurance under torture and realizing that their great strength and patience was from the grace and mercy of the one true God of the Christians, Claudius repented of his evil deeds and embraced the Christian faith along with his wife Hilaria, their sons Mavros and Jason, his servants and his soldiers.

When news of this conversion reached the ears of Numerianos, he was furious and commanded his men to tie a stone around Claudius' neck and to throw him into the sea. He also ordered them to torture the soldiers and to behead those who still refused to renounce Christ.

Mavros and Jason watched as Numerianos' orders were carried out. Instead of cowering in fear, they boldly stepped into the arena of martyrdom and stood before the tyrant.

"We stand before you, O Numerianos, and confess our faith in Jesus Christ, the Savior! We are not afraid to face our trials. Do what you will to our bodies; you will never destroy our souls, for they are in the hands of God. We will soon stand among His saints. Where will your soul stand, you impious tyrant?"

Numerianos was enraged by their fearless declaration of faith and issued the order, "Death by beheading for these two young fools! Execute them at once!" he ranted.

Shortly after the deaths of Claudius and the soldiers, pious Christians in the area took up their holy remains and buried them in a nearby cave. Hilaria later received the relics of her beloved sons and carefully placed them in a special plot that she frequently visited.

Her actions did not go unnoticed, however, and it was not long before she too was seized. Before being taken

Saints Chrysanthos and Daria

away, Hilaria asked her captors to leave her alone for a
few moments and, lifting her hands in prayer, the devoted wife and mother gave her soul to the Lord. Witnessing
this miraculous event, the executioners fled in amazement, leaving the woman's body where it lay.

When Hilaria's servants learned of the death of their
mistress, with much sorrow and reverence they placed
her to rest beside the graves of her beloved sons. Thus,
Claudius, Hilaria, Mavros and Jason were reunited and
together joined the ranks of martyrs before the throne of
God.

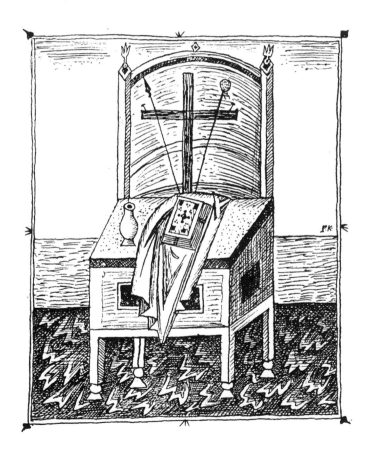

Saint Kalliopios

April 7

heokleia was a pious Christian widow who lived with her son Kalliopios in the small town of Pergi of Pamphylia, in Asia Minor. It was the end of the third century during a reign of terror for Christians. The cruel and godless ruler Maximos had issued orders for the capture and torture of anyone professing the name of Christ.

From birth the spark of faith had been planted in Kalliopios' tender heart, and by the age of fifteen it had become a flame of fire consuming the boy with a profound love for Jesus Christ. Despite the threats of harsh torture and death to Christians, Kalliopios did not shrink in fear. Instead, he considered it an honor and the greatest expression of love to die with the name of Christ on his pure lips. With all his heart and soul, he prepared himself spiritually through prayer, fasting and the holy eucharist to pursue his lofty goal. Kneeling before his mother, he received her words of guidance and her final blessing.

"My child," Theokleia began, holding back tears. "You have been called to confess our Lord and Savior. Do not be afraid, for He will stand beside you and give you strength. You are my son, the loving child of my heart, and it is with mixed emotions that I watch you depart. As a mother, I long for you to stay here in the shelter of your home but as a servant of Christ, I understand that His work surpasses my concerns as a mother. Go with God now and don't be afraid."

With tear-filled eyes she gazed at his face, trying to etch in her memory every boyish feature. She embraced him and kissed him one last time and clung to him before sending him on his way. With her words echoing in his ears, Kalliopios left his home for the last time.

Immediately, the boy sought Maximos out and boldly confronted him. "I have come before you, O Maximos, to proclaim my love for the Lord Jesus. You despise Him because you don't know Him. I, however, do know Him as King and God, as Creator and Master of the world and

all that is in it. You have treated his followers brutally and in your blindness are condemning your own soul to eternal damnation."

Maximos was astounded by the boy's daring and courage and in a rage commanded that he be seized immediately and brutally tortured. The innocent and gentle youth was subjected to the harshest of beatings with whips specially designed to inflict excruciating pain. This brutality was followed by slow, intense burns to his body.

Throughout the long ordeal, the

valiant Kalliopios said nothing. His answer to the mocking and vile sarcasm of his executioners was silence. His only utterances were humble words of prayer to his Lord and Master Jesus Christ to grant him the strength and patience he needed to endure his contest until the end.

The merciful God heard the prayer of his young servant and sent His angel to extinguish the flames which slowly singed his flesh, and Kalliopios was freed from his bonds. Theokleia was allowed to care for her loving son in the prison; his body was covered by blood-filled wounds. Although as a mother she was horrified by his torments, she nevertheless glorified God for allowing her son to be an athlete in the arena of martyrdom.

Theokleia stayed in the prison with Kalliopios, counseling him and encouraging him for the fight that still lay ahead. Mother and son prayed: "O Heavenly Father, you have always guided our footsteps. Hear the prayers of your unworthy servants and strengthen us as we are about to face the cruel torments of your adversaries."

As their prayers reached heavenward, a bright light suddenly appeared, illuminating the dark prison, and a heavenly voice acknowledged the boy's courageous confession of faith. Kalliopios and his mother were greatly moved by the divine vision and tearfully thanked God for yet another sign of His mercy and love. The Lord had fortified them with all the strength they needed to endure to the end.

When Kalliopios was brought before the evil tyrant the next day, he proclaimed his faith in Christ more zealously than ever before. Maximos shook with rage and issued the order, "Death by crucifixion!" It was Holy Friday of the year 294. Kalliopios and his mother accepted the sentence with deep humility and joy. She was so overcome with emotion when she heard that her son was to die on Holy Friday that Theokleia gave five gold coins to the executioners so they would not change their minds.

On the same day that his Lord and Savior had fallen asleep, Kalliopios, His pure and humble servant, closed his eyes to this world forever and received the sacred crown of martyrdom.

When the boy's precious body was taken down from the cross, Theokleia tearfully embraced it. "My child, my Kalliopios" were the only words that could emerge from her grieving heart. "You have won the fight. You have endured. May your journey be filled with light, my son. May the holy angels take you into His kingdom. Pray for me, your mother…the unworthy one." As she closely held her beloved child, her head dropped upon his chest, and she too surrendered her pious soul into the arms of her Lord Who united her with Kalliopios in His kingdom.

All who witnessed the scene of the mother and son were moved to tears. Even the hardened hearts of the executioners were deeply touched. Pious Christians collected the sacred relics of the new martyr and his mother and buried them side by side. Having faced death together, the loving mother and son together entered Paradise.

Saint Gabriel

April 20

I n 1684 in the village of Zverka, Poland, a son was born to the devout Orthodox Christian peasants, Peter and Anastasia Govdel. Named in honor of the Archangel Gabriel, the baby was baptized at the Zabludov Monastery's Church of the Dormition.

A pious, quiet child, the young boy spent much time in prayer and solitude and grew strong in spirit and in his love for the Lord. With his mature discernment, unusual in one so young, he helped others discern the will of God in their lives.

One day Anastasia prepared food for her husband. "Gabriel," she said, "I am going to the fields to take your father his meal. I will return quickly. Will you be all right in my absence?"

"Yes, mother," the little boy replied, "I will be all right. Don't worry. I'm not alone; God is always with me."

His mother turned and smiled at her son. She walked over to him and spontaneously embraced him and planted a kiss on his cheek.

"I love you, mother," said the small boy.

"I love you too, my dearest child." With this she shut the door and set out for the fields.

In her absence evil lost no time in striking. A demon-possessed tenant named Schutko abducted the boy from his home and led him to the town of Bialystok where he brutally tortured the child. After being tormented for nine days, his blood slowly drained from his body. Finally little Gabriel surrendered his pure soul into the hands of God.

To hide his crime, Schutko threw the tiny boy into the woods near Zverka to be devoured by wild beasts. When hungry dogs and vultures discovered the body, however, instead of devouring it, they protected it. It was Pascha and the blessed child was in God's care.

With the discovery of the child's body, the heinous crime was exposed. The townspeople were greatly horrified and saddened that such an atrocity could happen to one of their own.

Peter and Anastasia were grief-stricken. "Our little Gabriel, our baby! Why would anyone want to hurt him? He was our angel." With tears streaming down their cheeks, they took the remains of their small boy to Zabludov, where he was buried at the church cemetery.

Thirty years later, an epidemic killed thousands, and the bodies of many children were laid to rest near young Gabriel's grave. The people sensed a special grace and peace as they buried their sons and daughters beside him. It was during one such interment that Gabriel's coffin was unexpectedly uncovered and opened. To the amazement of all, the young body, after thirty years, had remained incorrupt. Recognized as a martyred saint, his sacred relics were solemnly placed in a crypt at the church of Zverka.

Many miracles occurred through the years at his gravesite and at the churches honoring him. For example, when a fire destroyed the church at Zverka in 1794, a portion of one of the saint's hands was burned. The people were greatly upset by the harm done to their holy child's relics and moved him to the Zabludov Monastery for safe-keeping. Their sorrow turned to joy and amazement, however, as they witnessed the burned hand had miraculously healed and was covered with new skin.

On Holy Pascha in 1894, the church that had been built at his gravesite to honor him was consecrated. Yet disaster struck again, only to be followed by another miracle for the edification of the people. Eight years after its consecration, the church dedicated to the holy martyr Gabriel was totally destroyed by another fire. This time, by God's intervention, the most venerated icon of the saint himself remained safe.

Many years later, tension caused by external strife forced the inhabitants of the Zabludov Diocese to send their beloved child-martyr to the Holy Trinity Monastery at Slutsky for safe keeping. They were later moved to Minsk and then, in 1944, to the Church of the Holy Protection at Grodno.

On September 21, 1992, they were returned to the Saint's homeland at Bialystok amid great celebration. The small reliquary of dark oak, adorned with roses, was carried in turn by clergy, monks, seminarians and laymen. Young children walked ahead of the young martyr's relics throwing flowers. A five-hundred-voice choir sang continuously, while fifty to sixty thousand faithful holding lighted candles followed the procession. After an all-night vigil, followed by the Divine Liturgy at the Saint Nicholas Cathedral at Bialystok, Saint Gabriel was finally laid to rest among the Orthodox Christians of Poland.

The pious, young martyr Gabriel, the beloved child of Orthodox Poles, is honored in his homeland to this day and remembered as the devoted child who intercedes for them before the throne of God.

Saints Rafael, Nicholas and Irene

Saint Irene

(with Saints Rafael and Nicholas)

Commemorated on Bright Tuesday

he story of a priest Rafael, a deacon Nicholas and a young girl Irene had been forgotten for many centuries by the inhabitants of Thermi, a small town on the Greek island of Mytilene. For centuries pilgrimages had been made on Bright Tuesday to the remains of a tiny hilltop chapel, but no one could recall why they went.

It was not until 1959 that the story began to unfold when the owners of the property began to build a new chapel upon the ruins of the previous one. During the course of construction, skeletal remains were unearthed which were gradually identified by visions of the saints themselves who began to reveal their story to a number of local inhabitants.

It was during the middle of the fifteenth century when the hieromonk Rafael and the hierodeacon Nicholas had set out for the city of Constantinople. However, before their arrival, news had spread that the city had fallen into the hands of the Ottoman Turks, and the destination of the two men was rerouted to the island of Mytilene (then called Lesbos). Finding their way to the Monastery of the Nativity of the Theotokos, Father Rafael and Deacon Nicholas settled in with Father Reuben, the monastery's only surviving monk.

It was there that the three monks peacefully lived a life of prayer, fasting, vigil and hard work until the year 1463, when the local residents of the island incited an uprising against the Turks who, by then, had seized and enslaved their homeland. The Turks immediately retaliated and sought to make examples of the perpetrators.

Basil, the mayor of Thermi, his wife, his daughter Irene, and a teacher, Theodore, ran to the monastery to warn the monks of imminent danger. On their way, however, the four Christians were arrested by a band of Turks who harshly afflicted them for hours.

"I know who you are," the spokesman of the group began, pushing Basil to the ground. "You are the mayor of Thermi. Give me the names of those responsible for this uprising immediately if you want to save your own lives!" he ordered.

Basil said nothing. He would never betray his countrymen. They all knew how greatly the townspeople had suffered under the Ottoman Turks, and they yearned to be free again. Even his twelve-year-old daughter Irene realized how greatly the Greeks cherished freedom and bravely supported her people's efforts to obtain it.

"You are a stubborn man, Basil, but I know how to make you talk," the Turk remarked deviously, his lips dripping venom. "Bring the child!" he ordered his men.

The brutal Turks along with a German mercenary began to torture Irene pitilessly before the eyes of her beloved parents. Basil and his wife were filled with horror as they watched the evil deed taking place before their eyes.

The Turks continued tormenting the child. Not only did they want the names of those who had incited the riot, but they also wanted Irene and her family to renounce their Orthodox faith as well. The Church had always been a great source of spiritual support and comfort for the Greeks who had suffered so much, and the Moslem Turks wanted very much to eradicate its existence forever.

The courageous young girl endured her suffering calmly and patiently, and turning to her parents said,

"My dearest parents, don't be sad. My pain will soon end, and I will be in God's Kingdom. He is here with me now. I consider it the greatest gift of my life to suffer for the sake of the Orthodox people and for my homeland. We will be victorious!"

Throughout her gruesome ordeal, Irene prayed. The end was near and she welcomed it, for she longed to be in the embrace of her beloved Lord. She surrendered her sweet soul into God's hands as she was burned alive inside a large earthenware jar. To the great fury of her captors, she never denied her Lord and Savior Jesus Christ.

The slaughter of her parents and the teacher immediately followed. A few days later, on the evening of Bright Tuesday, Father Rafael and Deacon Nicholas were also savagely martyred.

Today a women's monastery marks the spot of the early monastery and pilgrims piously venerate the sacred remains of the martyrs now housed within its walls—relics that for centuries had remained a secret to all, except to God.

Saints Kyriakos and Theodoulos

(with Saints Hesperos and Zoe)

May 2

When Katallos and his wife Tetradia left Rome in 125 A.D., they purchased at Pamphylia a family of Christian slaves—Hesperos, his wife Zoe, and their sons Kyriakos and Theodoulos. It was the reign of the Emperor Hadrian and a time of persecution. Although the family had remained Christian, their pagan owners constantly pressured them to worship the idols and abused them physically and mentally for refusing to comply.

One day Kyriakos and Theodoulos took their mother aside. "Mother," they said, "we can no longer live under these conditions. We are constantly pressured by our slave masters to worship their false deities. We are harassed and abused. We have remained silent under these attacks, but we will no longer continue to do so."

"I agree with you, my sons, but what can we do? We are their slaves. We have no voice," Zoe answered.

"We are slaves to no one, mother," the boys persisted. "We have been freed by the blood of our Lord Jesus Christ and are slaves to no one else but Him."

"You are absolutely right, my sons. We should have spoken up long ago. We must go to Katallos and plead our case before him. Come, I will accompany you."

Katallos looked up curiously as Zoe and her two sons approached, wondering why they wished to see him. Though their bodies looked tired and worn, their faces were full of life. Finally, he asked them, "What is the purpose of this visit? Don't you have something of greater importance to do at this time?"

"No, Katallos, nothing is more important than what we are about to say," began Kyriakos. "My mother, my brother and I have come to protest the harsh treatment we continuously receive at the hands of you and your wife. You know that we are Christians, yet you constantly pressure us to worship your idols. We refuse and will continue to refuse."

Theodoulos joined in, "You might legally own our bodies but you will never govern our souls. Our Lord and Savior Jesus Christ is the only Master we have and He is the only one we will obey."

Katallos was stunned! He had never expected such boldness from slaves. "I have the authority to kill you for your impudence and I ought to execute you on the spot. However, for the sake of your father I will give all of you another chance. Your father is a hard worker—one of the best slaves I own—and I have been very pleased with his labor. I will send the three of you to Tritoniun where he is working, for I am certain that he will be able to resolve this matter favorably once and for all."

What Katallos did not know, however, was that Hesperos was also a Christian. When he saw his family, he warmly embraced them and kissed them. After Zoe and the boys explained why Katallos had sent them to him, the four loyal Christians prayed to the Lord for guidance.

Time passed and Katallos and Tetradia prepared a birthday celebration for their son. They assumed that their Christian slaves had decided to accept the Roman gods and set out to test them. Sending the family meat and wine which had been offered to idols from the party, they waited to see if they would eat it. The Christians would not even taste the food but, instead, at the suggestion of the young brothers, threw it to the dogs.

Katallos went into a rage! "Torture them! Torture those two boys—those troublemakers! Hang them up and scrape their Christian flesh with iron claws! Make them suffer!" he ranted.

Hesperos and Zoe stood nearby and encouraged their sons, urging them to be brave until the end when they would receive the glorious crowns of martyrdom. Kyriakos and Theodoulos suffered greatly but remained firm in their conviction. At Katallos' orders, they were taken down and beaten severely together with their mother. Finally, the entire family was thrown into a fiery furnace where they joyfully exchanged their earthly lives for the Kingdom of Heaven.

The next morning when the executioners approached the furnace, they heard chanting from within and, puzzled, looked inside. They found the dead bodies of Hesperos, Zoe, Kyriakos and Theodoulos but, to their amazement, they had not been burned or marred in any way. They lay peacefully, as if asleep, facing the east.

God had protected His humble servants even in death and accepted them into His Kingdom. Freed from the bondage of their earthly slave masters, their souls were now united to their only Master, Jesus Christ, in Whose Realm they will dwell forever.

Saint John the Romanian

May 12

o a devout, peasant family of Oltenia in Romania, a son was born who was taught the precepts of the Orthodox Christian faith from an early age. The love for God, which was implanted within his young heart, continued to grow, nurtured by prayer and the Christian virtues.

In 1659 when John was fifteen years old, a band of Turks attacked the Olt Valley one autumn day and raided countless villages along the Danube River. Leaving a trail of destruction and horror, the conquerors rounded up the young people of the villages and took them as slaves. Among this group was John, who was taken captive and put in the service of a cruel, evil soldier. The young slaves suffered tremendously at the hands of their captors. They endured hunger and thirst, extreme fatigue and hard labor as well as beatings and any manner of human injustice the Turks could conjure. They even tried to force them into whatever unclean, lustful acts they desired.

One day a Turk tried to force John to commit a lewd act, but the boy violently protested. "You can never make me corrupt my body! My body is a temple of God and, as a Christian, I am required to keep it pure and unde-filed. I refuse to yield to your vile suggestions!" John said emphatically.

The Turk ignored John's protests and as he continued trying to force him against his will, the boy struck him in self-defense, killing him instantly. The other soldiers retaliated at once and, seizing John, chained him and subjected him to harsh torture.

Along with other slaves, John was taken to Constanti-nople. Bound and weak, he plodded along on foot and endured extreme exhaustion and pain. Arriving at the city, he was given as a slave to the wife of the brutal soldier John had killed.

Because John was a handsome youth, the woman was physically attracted to him and attempted to lure him into impure acts. In addition to this, she demanded that he accept the Islamic religion.

John boldly spoke up: "I will never do as you say. I will not give in to your sinful demands. You and other slaves of the flesh may consider your physical desires to be a natural part of life and therefore permissible under any circumstances. You are wrong, however. Such passions are only the product of a weak spirit that cannot control the flesh—a spirit that has lost its direction and the purpose of its existence. The society in which you live may condone such relations but my Christian faith reserves it only for those who are united in marriage. I am not your husband; you will not convince me to do what my Lord forbids. Don't waste your time expecting me to become a Moslem either. I will never leave my Christ! I will not live without Him. He is the only God— the God of truth and light, and He is the only one I worship and adore!"

Young John fervently prayed for strength to repel his mistress and to remain true to his faith. He preferred death as a Christian rather than life as a Moslem.

For his refusal to obey, the woman reported him to the authorities. The boy was immediately imprisoned and tortured mercilessly. Throughout his long ordeal, the young Christian prayed for endurance and courage until he was finally sentenced to death in the gallows. It was May 12, 1662. Young John, who had loved the Lord from birth, surrendered his soul into the hands of his only Master, Jesus Christ, and received the sacred crown of martyrdom, which the Lord has reserved for His beloved soldiers.

Saint Mark the New Martyr

To an Orthodox Christian couple—Andrew of Zakynthos and his Cretan wife—a son was born who was named Mark. When the child was eight years old his mother died, leaving him and his siblings in the care of their father who was sometimes very strict and abrupt with his children. Soon the father moved his family to Smyrna, where his harshness increased. As the abuse continued, young Mark could tolerate no more and eventually rebelled.

"I have had enough of my father's wrath," the boy thought to himself. "Things have changed so drastically since my beloved mother died. I will leave this house and forget everything about my miserable life here!"

Setting out to change his life, young Mark also left his Christian faith behind and became a Moslem, changing his name to Moustafas. His father was greatly upset by this decision, but no amount of pleading on his part could make the boy return to his Christian roots.

Time passed but Mark was still unhappy. He found no comfort in his new religion; it left him feeling empty and ill at ease. He missed the beauty of his Orthodox Christian faith; he longed for the mysticism; he longed for Christ. By God's loving mercy Mark came to his senses and traveled to Zakynthos where he entered a monastery and rediscovered his Orthodox Christian tradition. Leaving next for Constantinople, the boy found a holy parish priest, Father Meletios Syrigos, who fortified his faith and encouraged him in his spiritual struggles.

"I have sinned, Father Meletios," the youth cried. "I have turned my back upon Christ, my Lord and Savior. Can He ever forgive me for what I have done? How could I have been so foolish to think that I could find joy away from Him?"

"My child," the kind priest said. "Our God is a loving God. He is our Father, and like a good father, rejoices when his children see the error of their ways and return to the truth. He stands beside us always and only waits for us to invite Him into our hearts. You have done this now, young Mark. Don't be afraid. You are home now."

Mark shed bitter tears over his sins, but they were mixed with tears of great joy and love for Christ. He thanked the Lord again and again for helping him realize his great mistake and for loving him enough to bring him, the unworthy one, back into His fold. He was the lost sheep that the Good Shepherd had found and returned to the flock. And now on his road to repentance, he felt Christ, the Shepherd Himself, carrying him on His strong shoulders.

With tears streaming down his young face, Mark prayed, "My dear Christ, thank you for showing me how much you love me, the most wretched of all Your children. Take me by the hand and lead me wherever You wish me to go. Just stand beside me always so that I do not fall again. I need You in my life; my soul has longed for You…I love You, my Christ…I love You."

Mark prayed in this way for a long time. And when his prayers ceased, he remained on his knees, feeling the comfort and peace that only God can give. His happiness had returned; the great joy that only God can bestow moved within his entire being.

Fortified with prayer, Mark set out to appease his conscience and to openly confess his love for Christ. He returned to Smyrna where he loudly proclaimed his Christian faith and greatly angered the Moslem Turks by doing so. For his open confession, he was seized and brutally beaten, flogged and finally beheaded on May 14, 1643.

An eyewitness to the seventeen-year-old's martyrdom related the young Christian's last moments. Friends and enemies alike voiced their feelings—some wept, others jeered, others pleaded on the young man's behalf.

In the end, however, Mark was victorious. He had triumphed, by God's grace, and received the crown of glory. With joy in his heart, he had at last returned home.

Saints Kyriakos and Christianos

(with Saints Meletios, John, Stephanos, Serapion,
Kallinikos, Markiani, Palladia, Susanna and others)

May 24

Saints Kyriakos and Christianos lived during the reign of the Emperor Antoninus Iliogavalos who ruled from 218 to 222 A.D. They were young Christian children who saw their parents brought to the arena of martyrdom. As with many young saints, their own martyrdom is intertwined with the stories of other Christians whose deaths brought many to the true faith.

Saints Meletios, Stephanos and John served in the army. When ordered by the emperor to denounce their Christian faith or be tortured and killed, the three men unanimously chose the latter.

"Do you dare to disobey my command?" the emperor shrieked in disbelief.

"We do, O Antoninus," the three men loudly proclaimed. "We have one Ruler to Whom we offer allegiance, and that Ruler is our Lord and Savior, Jesus Christ! Even if you offer us all the glory of your kingdom, still we will not turn away from Him!"

"Then you shall indeed die for Him! You will suffer such pain that you will wish you had listened to your emperor!" Furiously turning to his men, he loudly ordered, "Take them away at once! Let them experience first hand the power of their emperor!"

For their refusal to obey the imperial command, the three Christians were beaten with thick wooden clubs, their ankles were pierced and their sides were ripped open with iron claws. Meletios was hung from a pine tree; Stephanos and John were beheaded.

Their commitment to Christ and their willingness to die for Him were not in vain, however. Others who witnessed their devotion to their Lord and Savior and their courage in martyrdom were brought to the faith. Among them was Serapion, an idolater. After witnessing Meletios destroy the pagan idols through his prayers to the Christian God, he renounced paganism and embraced the Christian faith with his heart and soul.

Another, who by God's grace became a Christian through Meletios' example, was Kallinikos, a magician. When attempts to poison Meletios failed to harm the Christian athlete, Kallinikos also accepted Christ. For turning their backs on the demonic gods and for their sincere devotion to the one true God, both Serapion and Kallinikos were beheaded.

Saints Markiani, Palladia and Susanna were among the women who bravely faced martyrdom with their children at this time. As countless other Christians who had stood before the emperor, they too were issued the ultimatum: "Either renounce this Jesus or be killed!" Antoninus shouted. The three loyal women did not hesitate for even a moment in giving their impassioned reply. "We love Christ, our Lord and our God! We offer Him our devotion and our very lives! We will never deny Him!"

It was now the women's turn to die for Christ. The soldiers savagely beat them and cut their flesh apart with wooden boards, yet through it all, Markiani, Palladia and Susanna did not waver. They met death fearlessly and joyously, again proving the superiority of the Christian faith and the power of Christ the Lord. The torturers themselves, however, were immediately punished for their brutal crimes against the innocent Christian women as their own lives came to a swift, harsh end.

Among the thousands of Christians who were tortured and slaughtered at this time were the toddlers, Kyriakos and Christianos, children of devout Christians who, in a few short years, had instilled in their tiny boys a great devotion to the Lord. Disregarding their young age and innocence, Antoninus called them forward for questioning.

"What can these babies know about this Jesus?" the emperor thought to himself. "These foolish adults refuse to renounce their God. I will get these children to obey my command and praise them before these fools who stubbornly refuse to follow my orders!"

Turning to the children, the ruler smiled. "Come, my children. You are such fine fellows. I have a question for you. Who is greater, the mighty Zeus or Christ Who was shamefully crucified? Now, answer loudly so that everyone will hear you."

The tiny boys, filled with the grace of God, smiled and replied sweetly and simply, "Christ!"

The emperor flew into a rage. "Take them! Take them away! These Christians and their children deserve to die! Kill them at once! Kill them as we did the others!"

Kyriakos and Christianos were immediately taken out and beheaded. Upon their tiny heads were placed the shining crowns of martyrdom as they joined their beloved parents in their Heavenly Home. They were among 11,000 faithful who were persecuted and together gave their lives for Christ. Though their mouths were silenced by martyrdom, their holy examples continue to inspire the beloved children of God.

Saints Claudius, Hypatios, Dionysios and Pavlos

(with Saints Loukillianos and Paula)

June 3

hen the aged Loukillianos, a priest of the idolaters, became a Christian about the year 270 A.D. during the reign of the tyrannical emperor Aurelian, he was taken before Silvanus, the governor of Nicomedia, who tried with a vengeance to persuade him to return to idolatry. Severely beaten and tortured for refusing to deny the Lord, Jesus Christ, whom he found late in his lifetime, he was then thrown into a damp, dark prison where he found four young orphans: Claudius, Hypatios, Dionysios and Pavlos.

Young and alone, the children had been thrown aside in the prison where only their great faith and love for Christ sustained them. It was this great love for the Lord burning within them that had prompted them to accept imprisonment willingly rather than a life without Him.

In the prison Loukillianos and the children spoke of God. "How great is our God!" the children exclaimed. "He loves us so much that He sent you to us, Loukillianos, to be with us and to help us. We are not afraid, for our good Christ is here with us, too."

They smiled sweetly as they spoke of Christ's love. They trusted Him and were not afraid. Armed with prayer and protected with the Christian shield of faith, the four children and Loukillianos, their new friend and guardian, were taken before Silvanus where they calmly and fearlessly awaited death.

The governor allowed them one last chance to renounce Christ, but to no avail. Nothing could tear them away from their Lord and Savior. Greatly enraged by their refusal to obey him, Silvanus ordered: "Throw these wretches into the furnace! Burn them alive! Let's see if their God will come to their aid!"

But Silvanus was ignorant of the power of God. As the martyrs were thrown into the furnace, a torrential rain suddenly appeared, extinguishing the flames, and the five emerged unharmed.

When this attempt at killing the Christians failed, Silvanus issued new sentences for the servants of God: crucifixion for Loukillianos and beheading for the children. Though orphaned and alone on earth, the children entered their celestial home where the Heavenly Father welcomed them in His loving embrace.

One who had followed the martyrdom of the four young children and the elderly Loukillianos was a young, devout Christian woman named Paula who for some time had secretly ministered to the needs of those Christians awaiting martyrdom in the prisons. After the martyrs had fallen asleep in the Lord, Paula collected their sacred relics, giving them over to the Church for proper burial and veneration.

For her Christian service to the five martyrs, Paula was arrested and brought before Silvanus. Refusing to deny the Lord, she too was brutally tortured and beheaded. So it was that Paula entered the Kingdom of God where she stands with the martyrs Claudius, Hypatios, Dionysios, Pavlos and Loukillianos before the throne of God and prays with them for the souls of those on earth who love the Lord.

Ὁ ἍΓΙΟΣ ΛΟΥΚΙΛΛΙΑΝΟΣ ΜΑΡΤΥς   Ἡ ἉΓΙΑ ΠΑΥΛΑ ΜΑΡΤΥς

Saints Loukillianos and Paula

Saint John the
New Martyr of China

June 11

hroughout China, during the Boxer Rebellion in 1900, there lived several communities of Orthodox Christians, holy branches of early Russian missionaries. Though few in number, they had worked diligently to preach the teachings of Christ among the vast sea of Buddhists, Taoists and Confucians. The tiny minority had remained true to its mission of spreading the faith and had never involved itself in the internal strife of the country. Nevertheless, their peaceful actions disturbed the Chinese revolutionaries who were suspicious of anything "foreign."

On June 11, 1900, a ruthless persecution began against the Christians throughout China, beginning with those in the city of Beijing. Almost all of the Orthodox churches were burned to the ground. Nothing remained of the Missionary Center at Peking; the fruits of many long years of labor were all destroyed, including the printing press and the library.

Unsatisfied with the destruction of the church's properties, the revolutionaries deviously planned to slaughter the Orthodox Christians themselves, beginning with the first Chinese Orthodox priest, Metrophanes Chi-Sung and his family. His wife Tatiana and twenty-three-year-old son Isaiah were killed before his eyes. Next, Father Metrophanes himself was stabbed in the chest by a violent group of rebels. Shortly thereafter, Isaiah's nineteen-year-old fiancee Maria was also brutally tortured and killed after trying to help other innocent Christians escape.

Father Metrophanes' eight-year-old son John was not to be spared, either. His persecutors cut him into pieces beginning with his nose, ears and toes, savagely mutilating the young boy. Throughout his gruesome ordeal, he never complained or protested, but he looked like an angel in the flesh.

As the young child lay dying, some witnessing his tortures pitied the boy and tried to console him. "Johnny," they said tenderly, gazing upon his mangled body. "Are you in a great deal of pain?" they asked, not knowing what else to say to him in his suffering.

The small boy looked at them sweetly and with a beautiful smile on his lips, which brightened his radiant face even more, he answered, "It's not difficult to suffer for Christ."

These words, filled with deep faith and love, were the last words to fall from his pure and innocent lips. Christ, Whom he had fearlessly and boldly confessed before his persecutors, welcomed His new child-martyr John into His Kingdom.

Following the martyrdom of John and his family, the teachers Paul and Ia Wang were also brutally tortured and slaughtered, along with hundreds of other Chinese Orthodox Christians. Together they were among the first Chinese people to shed their blood for Christ and His holy Church and to receive the most sacred crowns of martyrdom and eternal glory before God's heavenly throne.

Saint Aquilina

June 13

Aquilina was a lovely child who lived in the Phoenician city of Byblos with her father, Eftolmios, a well-known magistrate. It was during the violent reign of the Emperor Diocletian when Christians were being slaughtered by the thousands. Despite the danger, Aquilina was baptized at the age of five and was raised in a devout environment filled with prayer and the fear of God.

She was so pious and spiritually mature that, when she was ten years of age, she led her young friends to Christ. "My friends," she told them, "don't let the pagans deceive you. The stone idols they tell you to worship are fake gods. They are dolls made by men who don't know the true God. My God, the God of the Christians, is the one and only God, and He is the one I worship and adore. Turn to Him, believe in Him, and you will be saved."

Because her success at winning young converts to the faith was so great, an idolater informed the local authorities about her. The little girl was arrested and taken to appear before Volusian, the tyrannical ruler of the district.

Glaring down at her, Volusian began the interrogation. "Young lady, I have heard that you are a self-appointed teacher," he said sarcastically. "It seems that you have been telling your friends about Jesus, that crucified man. I am told you are urging them to turn their backs on the mighty gods of Rome and to worship Him instead. Is this true?"

"Yes, it is true and I will continue teaching the truth of Christ to them and to anyone else who mistakenly worships the dumb idols of Rome. Christ is God, the only Savior of the world, and I speak of Him with great joy. My friends are listening also because they know that I am speaking the truth."

Volusian became wild! He ordered that she be tortured in the most barbaric and inhumane ways possible. Beaten relentlessly, the child patiently and courageously bore even greater torments: she endured tremendous pain and agony when red-hot skewers were pierced through her ears. With blood streaming from her nose and mouth, Aquilina never denied her Lord. When at last the order to behead her was given, the triumphant child of God surrendered her pure soul into the hands of Christ. She had remained true to her Savior to the end, and for this she received the sacred crown of martyrdom.

Saint Vitus

(with Saints Modestos and Crescentia)

June 15

aint Vitus was born in Sicily and was the son of Gelas, a well-known dignitary. From an early age he loved the Lord so greatly that he began living a strict ascetic life of prayer and fasting. Granted the gift of healing for his ardent struggles in the spiritual life, the twelve-year-old spent his days healing the sick and converting many souls to Christ.

Valerian, the governor of the region, was not happy with the boy's lifestyle and confronted Gelas. "It appears, O Gelas, that your son is a Christian. I will not allow it!" He raised his voice for emphasis, "I command you to bring him back to our gods and to our way of life."

"I will try, but the boy is headstrong. He is so deeply involved with the followers of this Jesus that he refuses to listen to me," Gelas responded.

"You are his father! Make him obey!" snapped Valerian.

Gelas quickly ran home to find Vitus and to do as Valerian had ordered. He threatened, he coaxed; he brutally beat him, hoping to frighten him into obedience. The young boy, however, was not afraid to suffer for Christ and endured his father's physical and verbal abuse with patience and courage.

Summoned to the royal court, the child again proclaimed his faith—this time before the governor himself.

"So, you're the young Christian son of Gelas," Valerian said, noticing the boy's wounds. "You appear to have been beaten, young man. Could your father have done these things to you for refusing to obey him—and me?" he snarled, his lips quivering in anger.

"I will endure whatever I must for the sake of my Lord Jesus Christ!"

"Beat him! Torture him!" Valerian ordered. But as the words left his lips, his hand withered before his eyes. The governor was frightened. "What have you done to me?" he screamed.

Vitus pitied the man. Walking towards the governor, he prayed to the Lord, asking Him for a miracle. As the boy's intercession ended, the withered hand became whole again.

Astounded and terrified, but greatly relieved that his hand was cured, Valerian declared, "Send the boy home! Let him leave at once!"

Back at home, Vitus was subjected to a new type of coercion. Gelas was determined to bring his son back to the gods of Rome and surrounded him with an array of fleshly luxuries to lure him towards the secular life. The boy, however, fought off these temptations with the Christian weapon of prayer, and fortified by fasting. When angels appeared to strengthen the youth, Gelas was immediately blinded as he looked upon them. "What has happened to me? Help me!" the terrified man shouted.

The compassionate son came to his parent's aid. Just as he had prayed for Valerian's hand to be healed, he now asked God to cure his father's blindness. He hoped that his father, experiencing the miraculous healing firsthand, would embrace the Christian faith. Gelas, however, refused. Though no longer physically blind, he remained spiritually blind and secretly vowed to slay his son.

Modestos, Vitus' tutor, and Crescentia, his nurse, learned of Gelas' plot by God's grace, and they arranged to help the boy escape his father's wrath. Together the three Christians boarded a boat sailing to Lucania where they continued to live and teach the Christian precepts to the inhabitants of that Italian region.

News of young Vitus' gift of healing and teaching reached the Emperor Diocletian, who was eager to see the lad for himself. But his interest went beyond mere curiosity. His son was possessed by a demon, and he needed Vitus' gifts to cure him. Vitus was a sincere and loving Christian and as such greatly pitied those who suffered. Although he knew Diocletian's reputation as a brutal slayer of Christians, he nevertheless prayed and healed him.

Another miracle occurred but Diocletian—like Gelas—remained ungrateful. His hatred for Christ and His Church exceeded his gratitude. Instead of praising Christ for His love and compassion and thanking Vitus for his prayers, Diocletian responded by torturing the boy harshly for refusing to accept the Roman idols.

Young Vitus and Modestos were subjected to violent torments but each time the Lord came to their aid and delivered them unharmed. Scalding oil could not burn them and wild beasts refused to maul them.

Crescentia watched their ordeal from a distance. Inspired by their courageous acts for the faith, she came forward.

"I am a Christian too," she stated firmly. "These men are my fellow co-workers in Christ and I desire to suffer together with them!"

The Emperor couldn't believe what he had just heard. This Christian woman had just volunteered to die!

"Very well, then. I sentence you to suffer the same beastly tortures your friends here are experiencing! Guards! Seize her!"

With unceasing prayers, the three devoted servants of God once more prayed for deliverance. Immediately the earth shook, and many pagans died in the earthquake's aftermath.

Released from the godless tyrant by divine providence, Vitus, Modestos and Crescentia returned to Lucania where they continually praised God for His abundant love and mercy. Imploring the Lord to take their souls, they also asked Him to bless all who would remember them through the ages. In the year 303 A.D., Christ's loyal servants, who had willingly endured so much, peacefully surrendered their souls to their beloved Savior and joined the ranks of holy martyrs in His eternal kingdom.

Saint Nikitas the New Martyr

aint Nikitas was born in 1717 to Christian parents on the small Greek island of Nisiros. Although his father held a prominent position on the island, he was nevertheless accused of a crime by the Moslem Turks who had invaded, brutalized and enslaved the Greeks for centuries. His only chance to be acquitted was to become a Moslem—an act to which he conceded out of weakness and fear.

The ruthless Turks, however, were not satisfied with the conversion of the father only; they demanded the conversion of the children as well. The child who was baptized with the Christian name Nikitas now was forced to become a Moslem with his family and to accept the name Mehmet. The mother soon followed her husband and children and converted to Islam also. Though the parents were aware of their actions, the children were not and unfortunately were raised as Moslems without ever knowing their true Christian roots.

One day young Mehmet quarreled with a Turkish playmate. As the fight intensified, the Turkish boy's mother flew outside to investigate the matter. Offended that Mehmet was quarreling with her child, she angrily raised her voice at him.

"Who do you think you are fighting with my son? Do you think you are better than he is? You can never measure up to him!" she continued screaming. "At least he has always been a Moslem, raised by true Moslems! We're not like you and your family!" With those final words, the woman grabbed her son's arm and led him into the house.

Mehmet was left alone. He was puzzled by the woman's comments. Why would she say those things about him and his family? Just what did they do that was wrong?

He returned to his home at once and decided to ask his mother what the woman's words meant.

"Mother," the lad said, approaching his mother who was preparing the afternoon meal. "I was fighting with my friend, and his mother said that our family was different. She said that we weren't really Moslems. Is this true?"

Mehmet's mother looked at her son. He was very upset. She knew that she could no longer hide the truth from him. If she did not tell him the truth herself, then someday a stranger would present it to him in a very negative way.

"Your friend's mother was correct, my son," she began. "We were once Christians but were forced to convert to Islam." She went on to explain the reasons to her son as simply and sincerely as possible.

The boy was stunned! He had never imagined such a thing! How could his family have been forced to turn their backs on their religion and on their heritage? Though young, he knew their decision was wrong. He decided at once to remedy the situation.

"What was my name as a Christian, mother? I need to know!" the boy demanded.

His mother had no choice but to answer him. "At your Christian baptism you were given the name Nikitas."

"Then from now on I will be called Nikitas. I will answer to nothing else. Mehmet is dead. He never really existed anyway. He was just a lie!"

The young boy did more that day than return to his baptismal name. He made a commitment to return to his Christian faith and secretly planned to leave his home.

But where would he go? Who could teach him how to be a Christian? He needed to seek out other Christians and to live in a Christian environment.

By God's great mercy and love, the boy was led to the Monastery of Nea Moni on the island of Chios where the Abbot urged him to confess his sins to Makarios, the former Metropolitan of Corinth. He was then instructed and chrismated back into the Orthodox Christian faith— the true faith into which he had been born and baptized.

Though happy in his boyhood Church, he was still deeply troubled that he had once denied Christ and felt the need to confess his faith openly and to die a martyr's death. In order to strengthen himself for the arduous struggle that lay ahead, the boy, now sixteen years old, set off for a mountainous cave where he lit candles in prayer and prostrated himself before the Lord.

One day at the monastery, Nikitas tore off a piece of his clothing and offered it to the monks. "Use this rag to wipe off your hands after you light the vigil lights," he told the monks.

The monks were greatly puzzled by this bizarre act. But, they were even more puzzled when Nikitas retrieved the soiled cloth and re-sewed it back onto his garment.

Although the action was incredibly odd, the monks soon realized just how innocent Nikitas was and how much he loved the Lord. They recognized it as an act of great love and devotion and humility on the part of the lad who had, in his own way, presented a piece of his own garment—an essential possession—to the Lord's service.

Before pursuing his martyric goal, Nikitas returned to Nea Moni to seek permission from the elders. He knew the importance of obedience and was aware that he should never rely on his own prideful judgment.

The boy approached the assembled group of elders with great respect. "My fathers, I have led a sinful life. I denied Christ. For this I wish to die a martyr's death. I come to you, however, to obtain your forgiveness and your blessing before I pursue this goal."

"But you were a very small child when you converted to Islam," the Elders reasoned. "The decision was made for you."

"You are right. However, the sin still weighs heavily upon my soul. I will find no rest until I confess my faith openly and die for Christ."

The elders were unable to reach a decision. The matter was extremely serious. The boy's soul was at risk. Such a decision could only be reached through divine guidance. The elders came to a conclusion. "We must offer a Paraklesis to the Theotokos before giving an answer. God, in His infinite wisdom, will guide us to do the right thing."

The Paraklesis Service was offered. In the stillness of the monastery chapel, the elders and all the monks prayed. Nikitas himself fell to his knees and with tears flowing down his cheeks offered himself to the Lord in the only way that would appease his heavy conscience.

Nikitas prayed with deep humility. "My Lord, my Christ. How can I ever thank you for bringing me back to Your Church? You have given me more than just my faith; in Your infinite love and mercy You have returned my soul to me. You have given me another chance."

The small chapel was dark. The only lights penetrating the darkness were the vigil lamps hanging before the iconostasis and one lighted candle that illuminated the beautiful face of the Panagia, the Mother of God. Nikitas continued his prayer now to her.

"My dear Panagia, my sweetest Mother, please help me." His words, though not eloquent, were sincere because they emerged from his aching heart. All the pain of his young life came to the surface and spilled out before the Theotokos. She was the Mother of God but she was his mother as well.

"My Panagia, you know my sorrow. You know my wretchedness. But most of all, you know how much I love your Son and God. You know that I must die for Him. Only through martyrdom can I find peace. Deep down I know that this is the path that the Lord has chosen for me. If my request is wrong, please change the wishes of my heart. But if the decision is right, then please let the wise elders know. Help me, my dearest Mother, my Panagia. I will do whatever the Lord wants me to do. I will go wherever He wishes me to go. I will do His will, wherever it leads me."

The Paraklesis continued. As the chanting proceeded, Nikitas did not hear mortal voices. So involved in prayer was he that he thought he heard the music of angels instead. He was deeply moved and a great peace overcame him. He remained on his knees; and when the service ended, he knew the elders would give him the answer that was best for his soul.

The monks left the chapel quietly and reverently. They motioned for Nikitas to accompany them to the adjoining room.

"Nikitas, our spiritual son. We give you our forgiveness and our blessing. Do not fear, child. Be strong. Keep the Jesus prayer constantly on your lips. God will guide you."

Nikitas tearfully knelt before each of the elders. He offered a last prostration to each in turn and kissed their hands. As he knelt before them, they made the sign of the cross on his head. With this last blessing, the young boy quietly slipped out of the monastery and put his life in God's care.

It was not long before Nikitas was arrested. Penniless, he was unable to pay the haratzi (the head tax) that Christians were required to pay. The Crimean Moslem responsible for collecting the tax dragged him off to prison, but on the way stopped to arrest other Christians also. As Nikitas waited for the Crimean to round up the others, Father Daniel, an old acquaintance, passed by him.

"Greetings, Mehmet," Father Daniel smiled. "Why are you sitting here in chains, my boy? What have you done?" he continued, his expression changing to one of concern.

"I have been arrested for not paying the haratzi, Father," the boy replied.

"I didn't know that Moslems were required to pay that tax," he said in a puzzled tone.

Nikitas smiled warmly. "Father Daniel, I am most happy and grateful to our Lord, for I have returned to my Christian faith. I have never known such joy, Father."

Before he could continue telling his news to the priest, the Crimean who overheard the conversation interrupted harshly. "So, you have returned to your Christian roots, have you? You left Islam and became a Christian? What is this rebelliousness of yours? Come to your senses before I take drastic measures with you! Embrace Islam again and I shall forget I ever heard this conversation!"

"You heard me correctly," Nikitas affirmed. "I have returned to Christianity, the religion I was born into. I have returned home. I love Christ and intend to serve Him for the rest of my life!"

The Crimean turned Nikitas over to the authorities and for his refusal to accept the Moslem religion once again, he was severely beaten and thrown into prison. Gruesome tortures followed. He was bound and thrown into the stables that the horses might trample upon him, but the animals did not harm him. He was next thrown into a dungeon where he was subjected to extreme brutality for ten days and nights. Throughout his ordeal a brilliant light filled the prison and brought him great peace.

When these evil measures failed to convince the youth, Nikitas was thrown into a raging mob that pushed him, dragged him, beat him and cut him. Each member of the violent group tortured the boy as he wished. Nikitas, despite his suffering, continued to praise Christ and to confess him as the true God.

Taken to the outskirts of the city, the young Christian was given a final ultimatum. "Either become a Moslem or die!"

Without hesitation Nikitas chose death!

"If that is your choice, boy, then death it shall be!"

Nikitas was pushed to the ground. "Kneel, boy!" he was ordered.

Nikitas knelt.

"Bend your neck!"

Nikitas offered his neck.

The Turks laughed. They decided to make a game of this execution, hoping that the threats of impending death would terrify the youth into submission. For the sport of it they taunted him, forcing the boy to stand and then to kneel over and over again, each time flashing the sword of death before his eyes.

But Nikitas was not afraid. His lips moved in prayer, while he remained patient and calm. Christians witnessing the evil taunting prayed that the boy would not yield.

With great strength and courage, Nikitas boldly urged the Turks. "Put me to death so that I may return to Christ more quickly!"

The Turks were furious! The Crimean flew at the youth and, in a rage, struck him repeatedly with his sword before at last administering the fatal blow. On June 21, 1732, Nikitas surrendered his soul to His Lord and Savior Jesus Christ.

However, even the boy's death did not satisfy the savage Turks. To suppress the great respect and honor which the Christians bestowed upon the new martyr as they approached his body to collect the sacred relics, the Turks threw the filthy contents of a nearby cesspool upon the holy remains. Yet, to their dismay, they could not corrupt the young saint, because once the filth drained into the ground, the body remained immaculate and pure. Alexander Stouppis, a Christian at the scene who desired to save a piece of the newly martyred Saint, quickly approached the body and bit off a finger which he, in turn, presented to Saint Victor's Church. Determined that no other relics would be recovered, the Turks threw the holy remains into the sea.

The Crimean murderer did not go unpunished. His body began trembling and he soon received visions of the saint himself who beat him and frightened him so greatly that he had a stroke. At the urging of others, he painted an icon of the saint, which he kept in a cupboard. Although the nightmares and the beatings ceased after the icon entered the house, the Crimean remained paralyzed the rest of his life. His right hand that had struck the mortal blow was almost cut off by other Turks in a brawl and was rendered useless.

The icon did not remain hidden for long. When visitors heard knocking sounds from inside the cupboard, the icon was moved to another room where a vigil lamp was lit before it. The miracle of Saint Nikitas spread through-

out the region and, in time, more miracles attributed to
the saint occurred. Despite the injustice inflicted upon
His servant, the Lord transformed his death into glory.
What had once appeared as a victory for the Moslems
ended instead with their defeat! Nikitas, the young servant of God, had not only rejected Islam and embraced
Christianity, but also through the Lord's great mercy and
love brought others in search of the truth to Christ. The
boy who had once lived in darkness had led others to the
divine light.

Saints Lollia,
Probis and Urbanus

(with Saints Efstochios and Gaius)

June 23

During the reigns of Maximian and Agrippa about the year 300 A.D., there lived a man named Efstochios who was a priest of the idolaters. Having witnessed the courage and joy of the Christian martyrs and the miracles that happened during their contest, he sought out Evdoxios, the Bishop of Antioch, and was baptized into the Christian faith. He was soon after ordained into the holy priesthood and began spreading the word of Christ, the Lord.

Among those he taught were his nephew Gaius, Gaius' daughters Lollia and Probis and his son Urbanus who lived in Lystra, a town of Lycaenia. Not only were Gaius and his children baptized but his relatives as well.

For accepting the Christian faith and leading others to it, Efstochios was dragged by the pagan Greeks before the ruler where he was hung up and tortured. Taken with the children and their father afterwards before the ruler Agrippa, they were ordered to deny Christ. But the five devoted servants of the Lord dismissed the pagan's threats and remained true to Christ, their King and God.

Agrippa maliciously intended to make them suffer for refusing to obey his command. Beginning with the children Lollia and Urbanus, he hung them face-to-face and began torturing them so they could see each other's sufferings.

"Are you ready to denounce this Christ of yours?" he asked as each act of violence was inflicted.

"Never!" the children exclaimed. "Do what you will to us but we will never deny our Lord!"

Gaius, their beloved father, stood nearby regarding the blood his children shed for the Lord as a special blessing. After their agonizing trials, he too was harshly beaten and tortured.

Next, Probis was brought forward and shared the same brutal treatment as her siblings, father and uncle had. Beaten, pierced with nails, dismembered—they endured all for the sake of the Savior.

"Haven't you stubborn Christians had enough?" the diabolical tyrant asked, furious that all his brutality had produced no results.

"We have told you many times that we will never leave our Christ for your hideous idols. Finish with us so that we may join our beloved Lord!"

When, instead of denying Christ, they loudly proclaimed their faith in Him and called upon His holy name, they were beheaded. Lollia, Probis, and Urbanus, the loyal children of God, entered the Kingdom of Heaven along with Gaius and Efstochios with the sweet and immaculate name of the Lord upon their lips and will stand forever in His presence singing hymns of glory and praise.

Saint Eftropia

O n the list of Christ's holy young martyrs is included a twelve-year-old girl whose story is as brief as her young life. She comes to us as a beautiful rainbow that radiantly appears and then quickly fades away, leaving us in awe and with a glorious, lasting memory.

Eftropia was the young daughter of a Christian woman, Livy, who with her sister Leonis was martyred for her refusal to deny the Lord. Livy was beheaded and Leonis was burned to death. Little Eftropia was shot with arrows.

When the little girl was brought before the executioner, instead of being restrained, as was expected, her arms and legs were left free. It was the devious plot of the evil ruler to make it easier for the child to run away from fear and thus prove that she was denying the Lord God.

A mother's love knows no bounds, however, and even in her last moments, when her own earthly existence was about to end, two things filled Livy's heart—her God and her child. Unable to physically reach out to her young daughter, she called out to her, softly and sweetly and yet, with a mother's tone of authority, gently coaxed her to obey.

Eftropia fearlessly stood before her executioners with a quiet dignity and innocence that only the pure at heart possess. Her mother's words reached her ears: "Don't leave, my child."

The little girl looked at her mother and smiled ever so faintly. She obeyed her last wish for her and, putting her

hands behind her back, remained perfectly still as the
arrows flew towards her. She offered herself as a volun-
tary sacrifice to Christ and fulfilled a final obedience to
her mother, who soon joined her in death. Eftropia
accepted her mother's words, which were both a command and a blessing, and her most spotless and radiant
soul quickly soared to that glorious, angelic realm which
God has set aside for His beloved children.

Saint Kyrikos

(with Saint Julitta)

July 15

In the city of Iconium in Asia Minor lived Julitta, a pious woman of noble birth. Widowed while still young, she was left to raise her son Kyrikos alone. The greatest thing she taught the tiny boy was to love God above all, and this during the reign of the brutal emperor Diocletian, a wicked idolater and persecutor of Christians.

When large numbers of Christians were being massacred in Iconium, Julitta fled with her son to Seleucia, a seaport near Antioch, but the plight of the faithful was no better there. Again, in an effort to protect her baby, she fled to Tarsus.

But Alexandros, the ruler of Tarsus, was just as vicious as Diocletian and sought to put to death every Christian he could find who would not denounce Christ. Julitta and Kyrikos were among those arrested and brought before the governor.

Alexandros looked with curiosity at the woman who approached, holding a small boy in her arms. She was young and her demeanor indicated one of noble birth.

"State your names," he said dryly, proceeding through the familiar questions he had asked thousands of Christians.

"I am Julitta and this is my son Kyrikos," she answered, offering no more information than she was asked.

"I am told that you refuse to worship our gods. Is this so?" he asked.

"Yes, O ruler, you have heard correctly," she replied.

"Are you aware of the tortures that await Christians who refuse to obey the imperial command?"

"I am aware of the consequences," she responded, showing no signs of fear or intimidation.

"And you still refuse to renounce your crucified God?" he sarcastically asked.

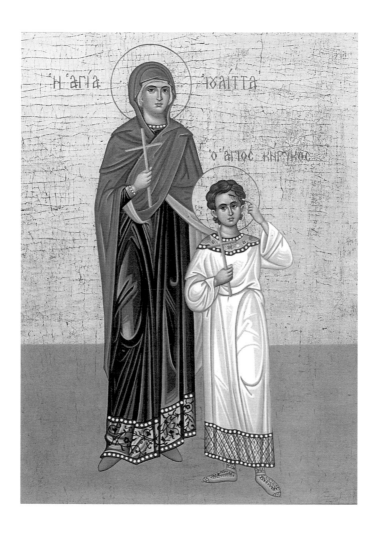

"I do. My love for Christ, my Lord and Savior, is unwavering. It is a treasure in my soul that I will keep forever. No imperial decree can change that."

Alexandros squirmed in his seat. He had become greatly agitated by Julitta's calmness and bold remarks. "Perhaps you can be persuaded to change your mind then." Turning to his men, he shouted, "Guards! See if you can persuade this young lady to consider my offer!"

Julitta and her baby were thrown into prison where the young mother was hurled to the floor and severely beaten. Bleeding profusely and barely able to stand, she was taken to Alexandros again. Despite her weakened condition, she stood before the ruler, her son in her arms, and again proclaimed her faith in Jesus Christ, her Savior.

Alexandros became angrier by the minute but tried to keep his composure in order to plan his next move. Her bravery had bruised his immense ego, and he could not let this young woman defeat him. He would find a way to make her comply.

Finally, he had an idea. "Let me hold your child," he said, reaching for the three-year-old before Julitta could refuse. "What a handsome boy he is," he added, stroking the baby's head. "What a shame it would be to let anything happen to such a fine fellow," he hinted, nodding his head deviously at the young mother. "Perhaps you may want to rethink how you feel about your Christ. Don't you agree, young boy?" he asked, glancing at Kyrikos.

The little boy looked at his mother standing in a pool of blood, her loving face wounded and swollen. He looked at Alexandros, the stranger who had hurt her. In his own way, he understood what was happening.

Showing no fear, Kyrikos kicked Alexandros in the stomach with all his might and said, "I love Christ!"

The governor became furious and like a madman threw the baby to the floor. As he rolled down the marble steps, little Kyrikos struck his head and there before his loving mother gave his soul to the Lord.

Julitta prayed that Christ would quickly bring her own trials to an end so that she might join her son in the Lord's Kingdom. Her prayer was heard. Enduring further beatings and torments, she was finally beheaded. It was the fifteenth day of July, 296.

THE PARABLE OF THE SOWER

Saint Marina
the Great Martyr

aint Marina was born in Antioch of Pisidia during the last half of the third century to Aidesios, a pagan priest, and his wife who died when the child was still quite young. Left to raise the girl alone, Aidesios put her in the care of a woman who was kind and decent and, by divine providence, a Christian.

Wise beyond her years and with a unique intelligence and goodness, Marina eagerly embraced the Christian faith. So greatly did she love Christ that with all her heart she desired to suffer for Him and to be counted among His martyrs. Wherever the young girl went, she confessed her faith and denounced the false beliefs of the idolaters.

Aidesios was greatly angered by his daughter's Christian faith and one day confronted her. "My daughter," he began, "why have you left our gods and devoted yourself to this Christ? Perhaps you have used poor judgment because of your youth, but I am willing to put all this in the past. Bow down now before our gods and we will begin anew. Forget this Jesus and his little band of followers and return to your senses."

Marina had anticipated this discussion for quite some time. She had known for a long while that her father despised Christ and fiercely disapproved of her involvement with Christians.

"My father, nothing you can say can make me worship your false gods. Can't you see that it is your judgment that is impaired and not mine? I will never leave my

Christ, for He is not one of many gods; He is the only God, and I will serve Him forever."

"Then you leave me no choice," her father stated, raising his voice. "Either you forget your foolishness and return to your home at once or I will no longer regard you as my child. Take some time to consider this matter carefully!"

"I need no time," Marina replied without hesitation, "for I made my choice long ago when I first learned the teachings of Christ, the Lord, as a very young child. I knew from then that I would always serve Him. The small seed of faith that was planted in my heart then has grown, by the grace of God, and has taken root in my soul. It is this faith that gives me life and I will not exchange it for death, which your demonic idols offer."

With these words, Marina turned and left her father's house. She was not dismayed, however. She was relieved, for she had confronted an obstacle that had stood in her way and now she was completely free to follow the Lord's will.

In time, the prefect Olymvrios received news of a beautiful fifteen-year-old who openly proclaimed the teachings of Christ. Upon seeing her for himself, he desired to take her as his wife, for she was indeed a rare beauty. Bringing her before him for questioning, he hoped to find out more about this lovely young Christian girl and convince her to renounce Christ.

Marina stood before the prefect calmly. "My name is Marina, and I am from Antioch of Pisidia. My greatest and only desire is to serve my only Master, Jesus Christ, forever!"

Olymvrios was astounded by her boldness. He still believed, however, that he could convince her to sacrifice to his pagan gods. Marina would not be swayed. Her mind and heart were firmly rooted in Christ and in His heavenly kingdom that awaits those who love Him.

For refusing to yield to the prefect's demands, Marina was beaten so severely with thorny rods that her blood soaked the ground beneath her. Yet God was with her during her struggle, giving her strength and patience to endure. More gruesome torments followed. Hung up and raked with iron claws, she was left physically broken and destroyed with blood streaming from her once beautiful body. Olymvrios could destroy her body, but he could not destroy her soul. With every breath left in her, she opened her swollen, bruised lips in prayer.

"My dearest Lord and Savior… I am in pain… My body is wounded and sore, but I thank You for allowing me to suffer for You." She struggled to continue. "I do not regret my decision to serve You… and I would be willing to die for You a hundred times more. I only ask You to always stand beside me, your unworthy servant."

Marina lay on the filthy floor of the prison, unaware of the new trials that awaited her. Before her appeared a horrific dragon the mere sight of which was enough to cause terror and trembling. Its sudden appearance startled her; however, she recognized him at once as the devil himself and immediately made the sign of the cross and called upon the name of the Lord. The dragon disappeared, but the evil one was not ready to give up yet and presented himself once again—this time as a hideous dog-like man, black and grotesque. Marina was not afraid, for she knew the mighty power of the Lord. She uttered the words "Jesus Christ" over and over again, which gave her strength and renewed her spirit. With the weapon of prayer, the young girl grabbed the demon and beat him with an iron rod. Trampling upon him, she conquered him with the aid of the almighty God and he vanished before her eyes.

At that moment a heavenly light appeared and a resplendent cross filled the prison with its brilliance. Above it was a pure white dove that said to her,

"Rejoice, Marina, for you will soon receive the crown of victory."

Marina heard the heavenly message and saw that her wounds were completely healed. With tears of joy and thanksgiving she prayed.

"Thank you, my dear Christ, for helping me in my hour of peril. You have strengthened me to slay the demon and have healed my broken body. You have filled my heart and soul with Your great love. Stand beside me

now in the last hours of my earthly life and have mercy on my wretched soul. Forgive whatever sins I have committed and cleanse me of every stain."

As she prayed with all her heart to her Heavenly Father, Marina was filled with joy. Her spirit was light and her love for the Lord swelled within her soul. The final words of her prayer flowed up from the deep recesses of her heart. "My Christ, I have loved You and will love You forever."

The following day, the young maiden again appeared before Olymvrios, who marveled that she had been healed. Nevertheless, he disregarded her declarations of faith and commanded that she be tortured even more—this time by fire and water. Many, witnessing the faith and courage of the young servant of Christ and observing how fearlessly and joyously she endured her trials, praised the one true God of the Christians and accepted Him as their own.

Marina's struggle finally ended when the godless tyrant condemned her to death by beheading. The young martyr, the courageous bride of Christ, joyfully bent her neck as a final sacrifice for her Lord and received from Him the most sacred crown of martyrdom and a place among the righteous in His eternal kingdom.

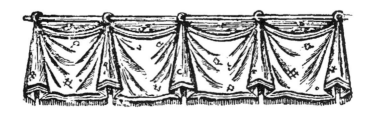

Saint Pollio

(with Saint Markellos)

July 18

arkellos Servilli Pollio was a child of the old, Roman, aristocratic family of Servilli. His father was a military hero who fell in battle and was buried with honors. His mother Cecilia became a devoted Christian after the death of her husband and raised their son Pollio according to the Traditions of the true faith.

They lived during the tyrannical reign of the Emperor Decius who abhorred Christians and unleashed an era of violent persecution against them. In order to practice their faith as they wished, Cecilia and Pollio took up residence with countless other Christians in the dark, damp catacombs that created a maze beneath the city of Rome. It was in this labyrinth where the followers of Christ lived, conducted services, studied the faith and buried their dead. Their priority was Christ, and for Him they were willing to sacrifice the sunshine, the fresh air and all the material trappings of the secular world to live according to His teachings. Only under the protection of night did a few venture to the surface to obtain food and other provisions for the underground Christian community and to claim the bodies of their martyred brethren.

Thirteen-year-old Pollio was among these volunteers who met contacts in the city who supplied food and clothing for the Christians. Along with the essentials, they also passed along news that was pertinent for their survival.

The story of young Pollio, however, cannot be told without including the conversion and martyrdom of Saint

Markellos who was a soldier in the Roman army. For his valor and military triumphs he was awarded the position of captain of the Praetorian Guard by the emperor himself. With his close friend and fellow soldier Loukoullos, Markellos conducted his military duties admirably, winning the respect and trust of those who served under him as well as of his superiors.

Though a military man by profession, Markellos was also a learned man who had studied various philosophers in his quest for the truth. Yet, no matter how much he studied, he still felt a great emptiness within himself.

One day Markellos and Loukoullos were among the spectators at the Roman Colosseum who witnessed the vicious slaughter of the Christians. This spectacle was common in Rome two hundred years after the crucifixion and resurrection of Christ, and the citizens of Rome made a sport of the evil and gruesome injustice.

As Markellos watched the Christians meet their deaths, he was struck by the manner in which they faced their final earthly moments. They were not only brave, but joyous and serene as well.

Turning to his friend, he said, "Loukoullos, how bravely these Christians face death. They show courage that I have not witnessed even among the bravest on the battlefield. Did you see that Christian gladiator's death? Although he had fearlessly killed two wild, starving beasts, he stood before the emperor and refused to kill a human being he could have easily slain! Imagine that!" he added, nodding his head slowly. "He would not fight a man because of his God!"

"Yes," Loukoullos added, "but look what happened to him. The man he refused to fight killed him instead! Where did his loyalty to his God get him? To the grave!"

"But, you must admit, he was extraordinary! Then there was that elderly man—the one barely able to stand—who heroically professed his God before a raging mob! His face was brilliant! I've never seen such joy in one whose life is about to end!"

"O Markellos, my friend," Loukoullos laughed. "Be careful. You might be mistaken as one of them!"

"Not I," answered Markellos. "But something about them still intrigues me."

The friends' conversation was cut short as the crowd's attention turned to a group of young Christian maidens who walked out into the arena. The audience anxiously anticipated their screams as the wild beasts attacked. What they heard instead were not terrifying cries but beautiful, sweet hymns of praise to Jesus, their Lord and Savior. Markellos thought within his soul that such music could only come from a divine source. As he watched the young girls, he again witnessed their peace and their joy—their great willingness to die for their Lord. Romans did not die this way. These Christians were different.

Markellos was greatly affected by this sight. The sound of their sweet voices echoed in his ears long after the maidens were dead. He must meet these Christians! He must find out how they died so happily and so courageously! What was their secret?

Without a word he left the Colosseum. He would find the entrance to these catacombs where the Christians hid themselves and question them himself.

Because of his reputation for accomplishing his duties thoroughly and meticulously, Markellos had been assigned the task of weeding out Christians and arresting them. He now had an excuse to leave the city and set out for the catacombs. Although the Romans knew the catacombs existed, they dared not enter them. The entrances to them were extremely difficult to find; and if they did find them, they were dangerous to enter. One who did not know his way through the winding corridors could very easily be lost forever.

Markellos set out for an area where Christians had often been seen, searching for someone to take him below ground. His sharp eye and quick military reflexes soon spotted and caught a young boy. With his authority as a military officer, he commanded the boy to lead him at once through the catacombs.

"I will not lead you anywhere!" Pollio boldly affirmed. "I will not betray my brethren!"

"You will take me to the entrance immediately!" Markellos insisted.

"You will harm them and I can't let you do that. Kill me here if you wish, but I will not take you to them. I would rather die than betray my Christian family! Torture me; kill me; do whatever you want!" Pollio shouted as he tried to free himself from the soldier's grasp.

Markellos was determined. He could not let this opportunity slip through his fingers. "Listen, my young man. I do not wish to harm your people. I only want to speak with them."

"Why would a soldier of Rome who murders my brothers and sisters every day only wish to talk? Why should I believe you when you kill us without a second thought?"

"You must believe me. I will not hurt them and I will not hurt you! Now, let's begin again. What is your name?" The soldier's voice was calm now and even friendly. His smile and pleasant manner put the boy at ease.

"My name is Pollio. But I can't take you underground because it is very dark there and I have no light. We will be lost."

"I have brought my own light, Pollio. Take me down to them. I will not hurt them. I give you my solemn vow. Believe me. I am the one who should fear. I am one and they are many. They could easily take me through the maze and lose me or even harm me in other ways."

Pollio finally agreed. Markellos had offered a logical argument. The soldier was indeed at their mercy. For some unknown reason Pollio trusted him and quietly led him through a hidden entrance and along the dark, winding underground corridors.

Markellos entered the catacombs as a pagan but within four days emerged as a Christian. His lifelong search for the truth had led him to the only Truth. His years of darkness ended with the light of Christ that illuminated his heart and soul. The emptiness that Markellos had felt all his life was now filled with the love and teachings of the Lord God. Among the subterranean graves of the Christian martyrs, Markellos found eternal life. He experienced a freedom he had never before known amid the followers of Christ sheltered quietly below the ground.

After being baptized by the priest Onorios, Markellos became a trustworthy and valued member of the Christian community and offered his life to them. Leaving his position in the Praetorian Guard, he took up residence in the catacombs and prayed and studied with his new spiritual family. At night he volunteered to join those who gathered supplies above ground and even offered to help ransom the bodies of the latest martyrs for Christian burial.

One day Markellos returned to the catacombs to discover that Pollio had been arrested. Cecilia, already in poor health, grieved for her beloved son. As a mother, she wept bitterly for her only child. In her fragile physical condition, she could not endure the profound sorrow and gave up her soul amid her friends and family in the catacombs.

Markellos set out at once to find his old friend Loukoullos who had taken over his own position in the Praetorian Guard. He knew he would help free the boy Pollio for the sake of their friendship. Upon seeing

Markellos, Loukoullos embraced him warmly and with genuine concern offered to help. His loyalty was torn, however. As a friend, he wanted to help Markellos and Pollio but as a soldier his aid was limited for he was required to fulfill his military orders. Markellos, who was also being sought by the Roman authorities, was nevertheless allowed to see Pollio and encouraged him to face his trials. The two Christian friends wept and prayed together, each supporting the other to endure whatever awaited them.

The next day at his trial, Pollio proved his unwavering devotion to the Lord. The Romans were no match for true Christian believers. The Romans offered earthly treasures; the Christians sought only heavenly ones. The Romans spoke of false, demonic idols; the Christians confessed the one and only God. The Romans threatened torture and death as an end to life; the Christians accepted them as a doorway to a new life in the Kingdom of Heaven.

"Young Pollio," the inquisitors began, "because of your youth and your fine lineage from the well-known Servilli family, we are willing to overlook your ridiculous beliefs in this crucified Nazarene if you return to the gods of Rome. You must honor your father's memory and live as he lived and honor his gods. Unfortunately, in her grief over her husband's death, your mother was easily lured into this cult of the Nazarene and took you with her, denying you your rightful place among the Roman aristocracy. You are the last of your great line, Pollio. Don't throw a bright future away. Come back to Rome that is willing to embrace you once more. Honor your family name."

"I honor my family and my name, sirs," Pollio replied, "but I honor and respect the Lord Jesus Christ more. There is no greater life, no greater reward than the one He offers in His Kingdom!"

"Don't be a fool!" the judges continued. "What has your crucified God ever done for you and your pitiful friends?"

"He gave His life that we might live. He shed His blood that our sins might be washed away. He gave us a life of truth. Without even knowing it, you enable us to receive great blessings when you persecute us, when you torture us, when you kill us, for you allow us to suffer for Him! I do not fear death. Do whatever you will to me. Burn me! Throw me to the beasts! How I die is irrelevant. It is only significant that I die for Him!"

"Then your wish will be fulfilled, you young fool! Rome has given you a chance to live, but you have chosen death!"

"No, Rome has offered death to my soul. My Christ has given me life. I choose eternal life with Him!"

Pollio was sentenced to death in the arena. With complete serenity and courage he walked into the Colosseum, oblivious of the crowd and the savage tiger that hungered for his flesh. Lifting his arms in prayer, his face shone radiantly as an ethereal joy lit up his countenance.

Markellos watched from the stands and stood up as the tiger pounced upon his young friend who had led him to his life in Christ. Immediately recognized by the Roman guards, he was arrested, to Loukoullos' great horror and grief. Despite Loukoullos' pleas to at least pretend to obey the Roman command, Markellos remained firm and gladly welcomed his turn to die for the faith that had restored his life.

Loukoullos was devastated as he watched his dearest friend slowly burned alive in the Colosseum. Never had he witnessed such valor from Markellos, even on the battlefield. In this new arena of battle—the arena of idolatry and vulgar secularism, Markellos distinguished himself as a true soldier of Christ.

Weeping openly, Loukoullos collected the ashes of his newly martyred friend and set out to bury them with honor in his own family plot. Before his plan could be executed, however, the priest Onorios gently insisted that Markellos receive a Christian burial and be laid to rest among the martyrs in the catacombs. At first reluctant, Loukoullos finally agreed. After all, Markellos had chosen Christ over Rome. At Onorios' invitation, Loukoullos entered the catacombs and witnessed the funeral and interment himself. Beside Markellos' grave lay the grave of young Pollio. The two soldiers of Christ would remain together in death. They had been victorious in battle. Truth had triumphed once more over falsehood; good had conquered evil; life in Christ had again overthrown death.

As an added blessing, Loukoullos became a friend of the Christians. Many years later, as an old man, he too was baptized. In his lifetime, Decius' reign ended and the Christians were free to practice the faith openly. Christ had triumphed—as He always will!

Saints Sekendos, Sekendikos and Kigoros

(with Saint Jerusalem)

July 26

Sekendos, Sekendikos and Kigoros were young brothers who lived with their mother in Alexandria, Egypt, during the last decade of the third century. Their mother, named Jerusalem, was a pious widow from a well-to-do but devout Christian family.

When she was young, she was extremely devout and rejected the secular life because she desired with all her heart to devote herself to Christ. Her parents, however, insisted that she marry and so she was forced to follow their wishes. The marriage produced three sons. Not long after the birth of the third boy, after only eight years of wedded life, Jerusalem's husband died.

The young widow raised her sons in a true Christian manner, teaching them not merely with words but, most importantly, by example. She herself began living a very ascetic life of fasting and prayer and frequent holy communion. She traveled with her boys throughout the area, teaching the word of God and bringing many to the Christian faith.

During one such journey, she met Efsevios, a pious hieromonk who became her director and guide in the spiritual life. Because of Jerusalem's great love and ascetical labors, the Lord bestowed upon her the gift of healing. So greatly did her fame as a healer spread that she was even called to Rome to heal the emperor's son.

Jerusalem and her sons traveled on, making several stops in Greece. Their efforts bore much fruit and the Church of Christ continued to grow.

In the year 276, Marcus Aurelius Probos took over the Roman Empire and another wave of religious persecution began. During this time, the fierce and ruthless Quintianos governed Thessaloniki, an area where Jerusalem and her sons were winning souls for Christ. It was to this beastly ruler that she and her young sons were betrayed.

Well aware of their plight, the young mother prepared her boys for the struggle before them.

"My beloved sons," she began gently. "We have been called to follow the path which thousands of pious Christians have taken—the road of martyrdom. It is a difficult path, my children, but it leads to glory." Jerusalem paused to look at her sons. They sat quietly and listened intently as their mother continued. "In our hours of suffering we must think only of the great reward that awaits us at the end—the loving, open arms of our Lord and Savior Jesus Christ.

"Never in our agony must we let any doubts enter our minds. We must think of the great Apostle Peter who walked upon the water to meet Jesus. His steps were firm until he doubted. Yet as he began to sink our Lord took him by the hand and led him to safety. Christ our Lord will be there for us too, my dearest children. He will take us from our sea of pain and lead us to His heavenly harbor."

Their struggle soon began. Demanding that the family be brought before him to face trial, Quintianos concentrated upon Kigoros, the youngest of the brothers. Though young in age, he was great in spirit and remained firm in his love for the Lord despite the flattery and threats of the governor. Hoping to frighten the rest of the family and, most of all, to weaken Jerusalem's resolve to remain a Christian, Quintianos subjected little Kigoros to the harshest of tortures. Placed upon a metal grill over a raging fire, the little boy accepted his torments without complaint and quietly prayed.

"My dearest Jesus... I can endure only with Your help. I will be strong... My dear Christ... hold me... help me...." He prayed such short phrases throughout his struggle—words filled with love and trust in the Savior.

Jerusalem could only stand by with her other sons and ask Christ to help them all endure until the end. Finally, the Lord took the child's pure soul.

Next came the turn of Sekendikos, the ten-year-old. Instead of trembling in fear after watching his younger brother's gruesome ordeal, he smiled as he bravely awaited his own sentence.

"I am happy to suffer for my Lord!" he proclaimed. "I love my Christ! I will never deny Him!"

None of the horrendous tortures that Quintianos could devise would change his heart. Nailed to the ground and brutally beaten, the child was then fitted with a fiery metal helmet. Enduring his afflictions bravely, he surrendered his soul to Christ the Lord.

When Sekendos, the oldest, was brought forward, none of the governor's promises of wealth, none of his persuasive arguments, none of his angry threats had any effect whatsoever upon the boy. Sekendos let him know immediately that he was cut of the same fabric as his two brothers.

"You think you have killed my brothers, O wicked ruler. You have only tortured and killed their bodies, but their souls are now free. They belong to God and have returned to Him. Free my soul quickly, for I too long to stand before my God!"

"You shall soon have your wish, you foolish child!" the governor shrieked.

After being dragged through the streets by wild horses, the lad joined his brothers before the Lord.

Jerusalem, ready to face her own martyrdom, thanked God for strengthening her sons in their struggles and for honoring them with crowns of victory. Her tortures were so brutal that witnesses openly wept for the young mother who, having suffered through witnessing the torments of her sons, now suffered through her own trials. She was finally beheaded and her soul was set free to join her beloved Sekendos, Sekendikos and Kigoros as they stood before the Lord in His kingdom.

The Three Holy Sons of Saint Theodote

(with their righteous mother)

July 29

Saint Theodote was a pious widow who lived with her children in the city of Nicaea. Extremely beautiful, the young woman was approached by many men of the town who sought her hand in marriage. The loving mother, however, was not interested in a second marriage, for her only concern was to raise her three boys properly and according to the teachings of Christ.

Life was not easy for the young family. It was the period of iconoclasm, a movement committed to removing and destroying the holy icons from every part of the Byzantine Empire. Devoted to the Church and understanding the importance of icons in worship and in the lives of all Christians, Theodote and her sons were among the first to speak out in their support and worked diligently to turn the inhabitants of the region against the iconoclastic emperor and his followers. In order to enlighten as many people as possible, Theodote approached the women of the town while her sons dealt with their own peers.

"Dear friends," the boys addressed the young people of Nicaea. "We are members of Christ's great Church. As you know, there is a movement astir that wants to destroy our sacred icons. We cannot let this happen. Many ignorant and false statements have been made to convince our people that the icons should be removed from our churches. They refer to them as 'idols.' They say we are worshiping these 'idols' instead of our God. But they are trying to deceive us."

The crowd that had gathered listened intently to the words of the young men before them. They spoke eloquently and sincerely as well as with authority. Even adults stopped to hear their words and were impressed.

The boys continued. "Listen, don't be misled. We only worship our God. We do not worship these images of Him, of the Theotokos and of the saints; we only venerate them. Through them we honor the holy ones they depict. Holy icons are not idols; God did not prohibit them in His Commandments that He gave to Moses centuries ago on Mount Sinai. Didn't our Lord command that images of the Cherubim be placed upon the curtains of the tabernacle and upon the mercy seat? Didn't He appear to us in the flesh as Jesus, the

Christ? It is because of His Incarnation that we can have images of Him.

"Friends and fellow students, do we not speak the truth here today? Our icons are a very important part of our worship services. Close your eyes for a moment and think of the icon you love the most—the one you pray before in your rooms at night. Doesn't it turn your mind and your heart heavenward? Doesn't it give you a glimpse of heaven? Our God in His great wisdom has taken the simple things of the earth—wood and paint—and has sanctified them. Only our great God can do that. He has given them to us as sacred tools that we can use to grow ever closer to Him. Can't you see their great value in our lives?"

Many in the huge crowd who had gathered nodded their heads in agreement. However, others who rejected the icons also lurked about, gathering as much information as they could against those who spoke out in favor of them.

Soon Theodote and her children were arrested and tortured. The family was not afraid, however, and instead considered it an honor to suffer for the faith. They knew that God's divine will would be done in the end, despite the efforts of those who fought against it. God would prevail. He always does. Theodote and her sons thanked God for giving them the proper words to do His work. They humbly thanked Him for allowing them to serve Him.

Mother and sons were sentenced to death and together received the sacred crowns of martyrdom. Later a church was built to honor their heroic struggles and unwavering devotion to Christ and the triumph of His holy Orthodox Church.

Saint Elesa

August 1

aint Elesa was the child for whom her devout mother Evgenia had prayed. Because she had been unable to conceive, the woman promised that, if her prayer was answered, she would dedicate the child to the Lord.

One day she heard a heavenly voice which told her that, through God's mercy, she would soon bear a child. Evgenia was filled with joy and glorified God when she and her husband Elladios, a wealthy magistrate, held a beautiful baby daughter in their arms at last. They named the infant Elesa from the Greek word meaning mercy.

The infant was soon baptized and was taught the Christian virtues by her mother. Living a life of prayer, fasting and almsgiving, the girl grew closer to God Whom she loved with all her heart and soul.

But Elladios, an impious idolater, detested the fact that his daughter was a Christian. He had only tolerated Christianity through the years for the sake of his wife whom he loved dearly. Time, however, brought change. When Elesa was fourteen years old, her beloved mother became seriously ill. Feeling her earthly days coming to an end, Evgenia called her daughter to her bedside. Elesa quietly approached, took her mother's frail hand in hers and tried to hold back her tears.

"My darling daughter, my Elesa. You have been the greatest joy of my life. You are the child wrought by prayer—the most blessed gift to your parents from our merciful Father in Heaven. When I first held you in my arms, I wept tears of great joy. You were the most beautiful baby I had ever seen and you were so greatly loved."

Both mother and daughter smiled through their tears. "Yours will be the last face I shall see in this world. Soon I shall leave you...."

"No, my mother," Elesa interrupted. "You will get better; I will take care of you. Don't leave me now!" The girl wept bitterly, her tears trickling softly upon her mother's hand.

"Don't cry, my dear Elesa, for it is time for me to return to my heavenly home. Promise me one thing: Promise me that you will remain true to our Lord Jesus Christ Who has bestowed so many blessings upon us. Stay close to Him for the rest of your life. Only then will I be able to leave you in peace. He will be with you, my daughter... He will take care of you... And I... from the other world will pray for you always."

"Don't worry, mother. Your promise will not be difficult to keep. I love our Christ with all my heart and I long to devote my life to Him."

Evgenia smiled weakly. Her life was slipping away, but she was serene. "I give you my blessing... my dearest child.... Go with God...my Elesa... my Elesa...."

In the peaceful silence, Evgenia closed her eyes to this world forever. Elesa embraced her mother and wept.

In her grief the young girl prayed, "O Lord Jesus Christ, please accept in Your Kingdom the beautiful soul of my sweet mother. And be with me, my dear Christ... I need You now more than ever."

Both Elladios and Elesa grieved for the beloved wife and mother. Nothing would ever be the same again for either of them.

Time passed and Elladios decided that Elesa should marry. Of all the maidens throughout southern Greece, Elesa was among the most beautiful, the most virtuous and most wise. Finding a good mate for her would not be difficult, for many sought her hand in marriage. The young girl, however, did not desire an earthly bridegroom—she longed for her heavenly Bridegroom and gave excuses for not choosing a husband.

When Elladios left for a trip, Elesa found the perfect opportunity to flee from her home. After asking God to direct her path, she boarded a ship with two maidservants and sailed for Kythera, a remote island well suited to the ascetic life.

As the ship's crew helped the maidens unload their possessions, a poisonous snake suddenly bit one of the seamen. Within a few moments, to everyone's horror he was dead. Elesa was called to the scene. Having compassion on him, she fervently prayed to the Lord and made the sign of the cross over him. By God's mercy, the man was brought back to life. When the ship returned to the village, the seamen told everyone they met about Elesa and the great miracle that had occurred through her intercession.

Soon Elladios returned home, expecting to find his daughter and planning to pursue further the task of finding her a husband. Annoyed by her absence, he became even more enraged when he learned that Elesa and two handmaidens had distributed their wealth among the needy and had set sail for an unknown destination to live as Christian ascetics.

Finding the captain of the ship, Elladios angrily shouted, "Where have you taken my daughter?"

The man did not want to answer but Elladios persisted. "Where is Elesa?" he asked again, this time grabbing the frightened man by the throat. "Take me to her immediately!"

The captain turned his ship around and sailed back to Kythera. Once there, Elladios set out to find Elesa and her servants and finally discovered them in a secluded spot atop a high mountain. Although he pleaded with his daughter and tried every means possible to convince her to return back to their village with him, she would not change her mind. The more he urged her to leave the island, the more she affirmed her intention to stay.

Elladios could hide his rage no longer. His eyes bulging in anger, he turned his wrath upon the young girl. "How dare you leave your home! And what did you leave it for? This remote wilderness with nothing but savage beasts! You ungrateful girl! Is this how you repay your father who has given you everything!"

Elesa would not budge. "Tell me," Elladios continued ranting and raving. "Why won't you return to your home?"

Elesa boldly replied. "I will give you the answer to this question, Father. I will tell you exactly why I left my home and will never return to it again. It is because you are there!"

Elladios was seething as he stared at Elesa in disbelief. How dare she talk to him like this!

Despite the rage in her father's face, Elesa continued. "I am a Christian and will always be a Christian! I will not live in a house of idolaters who worship worthless, man-made idols, and I will never again live in a pagan household where idolatry prevails! I prefer instead to live in the beauty of this remote island in the presence of wild beasts!"

The madman could hear no more. He seized Elesa and began beating her savagely. Her servant, in terror, could only stand and watch. The girl quietly accepted her suffering and prayed. After more torments, Elesa fell to the ground dead.

However, by the mercy of God, she arose from the dead and praised and thanked the Lord for allowing her to suffer for Him. She also asked that He grant the request of anyone who prays for her intercession.

Her supplications further infuriated her father. He chased Elesa like a wild beast after its prey, ready to stone her. Immediately the mountain parted, allowing her to pass. Nevertheless, Elladios soon overtook her and inflicted the final blow. Leaving her dead, he dragged one of the servant girls with him to the waiting ship and sailed for home.

The other handmaiden, emerging from her hiding place, buried the holy remains of her beloved Elesa high atop the mountain, which even today is known as St. Elesa's Mountain. For several nights she witnessed a heavenly light and heard the hymns of angels above the sacred tomb.

Later a town was established on the island, and to this day devout pilgrims offer prayers at the Church dedicated to Saint Elesa. The rock, which miraculously opened before her as she fled from her father, still serves as a reminder of the saint's great love and sacrifice for her Lord and Savior. Elesa had kept her promise to her mother—she had remained true to the Lord... until the end of her life.

The Seven Youths of Ephesus

(Saints Maximilianos, Exakoustodianos, Iamblicus,

Martinianos, Dionysios, Antonios and Konstantinos)

August 4

even brothers lived in Ephesus in 252 A.D., children from a pious, well-to-do Christian family. Not long after their baptism, the boys were orphaned. Decius, the emperor of Rome at the time, knew the family well but was extremely upset when he found out that they had embraced Christianity. When their parents died, he found the perfect excuse to visit the boys with the intention of luring them back to paganism.

The boys feared the emperor's motives, for they knew they would never deny the one true God. Their only alternative was to leave Ephesus. Distributing all their material possessions to the poor, the boys, ranging from eight to fifteen years of age, fled the city and found refuge in a cave. Hidden away in their new shelter, the brothers were determined to stay together and remain true to the faith. With this common resolve, they prayed fervently to God for His mercy and guidance. That night, as they slept, the Lord took their pure souls into His care.

One hundred ninety-four years passed and the boys' plight had been forgotten long since. It was 446 A.D. and, although the days of Christian persecution had ended, a new heresy plagued the Christian Church from within. Many of the clergy and the laity no longer accepted the resurrection of the dead, and those who did proclaim it were imprisoned.

Theodosius the Less ruled the empire at that time. A God-fearing man, he championed the Orthodox teachings of the Church and pleaded with God to help him deal with the crisis before him.

One day a wealthy landowner began building a stone enclosure for his sheep. Since he needed all the stones he could find, he took apart the stone wall that sealed the entrance of a nearby cave, unaware of what had occurred there centuries before. When the cave was opened, by God's providence, the brothers were resurrected. Upon awakening, however, they were completely unaware of the passage of time and assumed that they had just risen from a good night's sleep.

Maximilianos, as the oldest, took charge of all matters. Realizing that their provisions were low, he gave Iamblicus money to return to the city to purchase supplies and also determine the whereabouts of Decius.

Iamblicus cautiously set out for Ephesus. As he entered the city, he was bewildered by the changes he saw and thought perhaps that he was having a vision. Stopping to buy bread, he paid for it with the money Maximilianos had given him.

The merchant stopped Iamblicus and looked again at the money in his hands. "What are these coins you have given me, boy?" he asked, curiously turning the coins over in his hand for a better look.

"Didn't I give you enough money, sir?" the boy innocently asked. "Do I owe you more?"

"You know exactly what I mean," the merchant said. Look at them! They're worth a fortune! Now tell me, where did you get them?"

Iamblicus was stunned. "My brother gave me these coins to buy supplies."

"Look, young man, tell me where this treasure is!" the man persisted. "I demand that you tell me at once! Either tell me and let me have a share of the wealth, or I will turn you over to the authorities! Now, where is the treasure?"

"But I have already told you—there is no treasure," the boy replied. "The coins belong to my brothers and me."

The greedy merchant would not listen. Convinced that Iamblicus was hoarding a treasure, he put him in chains

and dragged him through the streets to the proconsul of Ephesus for interrogation.

Throughout the questioning Iamblicus held to his story.

"Where are you from?" the proconsul asked.

"Ephesus, sir. I will even give you the names of my parents who were well known here before their deaths not long ago. Many people knew them and know my brothers and me as well."

Iamblicus stated the names of his parents and gave a few details of their lives but the group of men standing about him was greatly bewildered.

"Come now, young man. We've heard enough of your lies. All of us were born here in Ephesus and have lived here all our lives and we've never heard of your parents. It's time you tell the truth!"

"But I am telling the truth! Why won't you believe me?" The boy exclaimed.

The men began talking among themselves while Iamblicus patiently waited. Still interested in finding out where the Emperor Decius was, he asked. "Tell me please, is Decius still in the city or has he already left?"

The men stared at him in disbelief. "Are you crazy, boy?" they asked, totally mystified by his question. First, you produce valuable coins etched with the image of the Emperor Decius who has been dead for two hundred years and then you ask us if he is still in the city! What kind of joking is this?"

Iamblicus could not respond. No matter what he said, they would not believe him. He wondered why they had told him Decius had been dead for two hundred years. Why, he was still alive. He and his brothers had just fled from him the day before.

Finally Marinos, the Bishop of Ephesus, suspected that a supernatural event had occurred and suggested that the boy lead them back to his brothers. As they approached the cave, to their amazement they found clues that supported the authenticity of the youngster's story.

A sheath was found at the entrance to the cave containing two seals which, according to its inscription, had been placed there by two Christians, Rufinos and Theodore. Decius had sent them to seal the entrance to the cave where the dead bodies of the boys had been found back in the third century. The names of the brothers and the details of their deaths had also been inscribed on the leaden tablets.

During the time of persecution the Church had ordered that the names of those martyred for the faith and details of their martyrdom be preserved along with their sacred relics. By doing so, the Church could honor them and the faithful would be inspired by their struggle.

Proceeding deeper into the cave, they found the six other brothers alive and well. The bishop, the proconsul and all in their company tearfully bowed in awe, realizing that they were in the presence of saints who had been resurrected. And this at a time when the resurrection of the dead was being denied!

The Emperor Theodosius was summoned and, rushing to Ephesus, fell before the feet of the saints. As they spoke together, the boys became weary, and there before the emperor and the other witnesses they gave up their souls to God.

Theodosios ordered elaborate clothing and coffins of gold and silver for the brothers. But that night the saints appeared to him in a dream.

"Your Highness, we humbly ask that you grant our request. We do not want gold and silver. These are the treasures of earth. The only worthwhile treasure is found in the Kingdom of Heaven. Please leave our mortal remains in the cave where we, as martyrs, fled from the emperor's wrath and surrendered our souls to the Lord."

News of the resurrected saints spread throughout Ephesus. Theodosius ordered great celebrations and, in honor of the seven brothers, donated large sums of money to the poor. All the clergy and laymen who had been imprisoned for defending the truth were released.

The debate concerning the resurrection of the dead ended. Seven pure and innocent young brothers had been used to reveal a great mystery. God Himself had intervened.

Saint Triantafyllos

August 8

Saint Triantafyllos lived in the middle of the seventeenth century and was born in Zagora near the city of Volos in northern Greece. It was a time of slavery for the Greeks, as they suffered severely under the domination of the Turks. Christians were a prime target for the Moslem Turks and often without cause they would provoke issues in order to torture and condemn to death those who would not embrace Islam.

Triantafyllos was working as a seaman, and when he was only fifteen years old the Turks arrested him for no apparent reason.

"Where are you taking me," the bewildered boy asked. "What have I done? I have broken no laws!"

The Turks would explain nothing to him as they dragged him away. Turning him over to higher authorities, they pressured him to renounce Christ.

Triantafyllos, finally understanding that he had been seized only because he was a Christian, remained firm. "I will never do as you ask! Kill me if you must! You can torture me until I can no longer stand up but I will not leave my Lord."

On August 8, 1680, Triantafyllos met a martyr's end at the hands of the cruel Ottoman Turks. However, God rewarded the youth's sacrifice of love; from his holy remains a beautiful fragrance arose—a sign of true blessedness. The holy Church commemorates Saint Triantafyllos on the eighth day of August.

Saints Theognios, Agapios and Pistos

(with Saint Vassa)

August 21

In the city of Edessa at the end of the third century there once lived a pious young woman named Vassa. When she was young, she learned the teachings of Christ from her devout Christian family and lived her life faithfully with the fear of God.

When she became of age, she married Valerian, a pagan priest, and gave birth to three sons: Theognios, Agapios and Pistos. As a true servant of the Lord, Vassa raised her sons as Christians and passed on to them her own great respect and love for Jesus Christ the Savior.

Unfortunately, Valerian despised Christianity and, even more, loathed the fact that his wife and sons embraced the teachings of Christ. Although Vassa had suffered at his hands for years, she would still not give up her Lord and God.

One day the diabolical husband flew into a rage. "I have had enough of this Christ of yours. Not only do you worship Him but you have brainwashed our sons with His teachings too! You are ruining my life! I have had enough of this cult of the Nazarene! Why can't you obey your husband for a change and worship my gods, the gods that all of Rome worships?" he fumed, his face turning a fiery red.

"I will not worship your gods, my husband, because they are demons. You are proof enough that they are false, for I see how your worship of them corrupts you more and more with each passing year. I look at you and see only hatred and cruelty. My Christ, the true God, the only God, bestows upon His devoted followers the gifts of tranquility and compassion and love. I pity you, Valerian; I pity your miserable soul. But I shall pray for you always."

Even more infuriated by his wife's calm reply, Valerian turned Vassa and their sons over to Vicarius, the governor of the area. "I have been living with a household of Christians, O governor," Valerian complained, "and I can tolerate no more of their prayers and their hymns. Do with them as you see fit!"

Vicarius immediately issued strict orders to have Vassa and her boys brought before him. When the four admitted openly and fearlessly that they were indeed Christians and declared their loyalty to Christ forever, the governor was furious. He tried every means possible to force them to sacrifice to the hideous idols of Rome, but nothing worked; mother and sons would never forsake their Lord.

In order to weaken Vassa, Vicarius ordered that Theognios, the oldest son, be tortured mercilessly before the eyes of his family. Though he was hung up and his flesh was torn to shreds, the boy would not deny his Christ.

Vassa was horrified by the gruesome scene before her eyes. However, her beloved Theognios, her firstborn, remained serene and prayed throughout his agony. He had learned his lessons well at her knee and never once complained or called out in anger against his persecutors.

The loving mother prayed for him to endure. "Be patient, my child, be strong. Very soon you will be with our Lord. You will know His peace; you will experience His joy."

When Vicarius realized that his evil scheme was not working and that Theognios had remained firm in his faith, he ordered even harsher tortures for Agapios, the second son. With whips and knives, the godless beasts tormented the young lad for hours; his skin was ripped from his head to his chest. Vassa, with a mother's heart, watched her child and prayed. She offered him hope and encouragement, reminding him also of the great reward that awaited him in God's Kingdom.

Agapios, despite his suffering, proclaimed loudly enough for all to hear, "Nothing could be sweeter or more beautiful than for one to suffer for Christ!"

Pistos, the youngest, was called next. Although the smallest, he was nevertheless equally as strong and courageous as his two older brothers. Beaten and tortured, he remained true to his Lord.

"You have tortured my brothers, you cruel beast, and by doing so think that you have frightened me since I am the youngest. I love my Christ too, and you will see that I will continue loving Him no matter how brutally you torment me. My father worshiped your false idols; I will not!"

Vicarius was enraged. "These three small brothers have defied me! None of my torments has turned them back to the Roman gods! They stubbornly cling to this Christian deity of theirs!" He ranted on and on, growing angrier by the minute. "Death by the sword for all three of these young fools!"

Before the sun had set that day, the three devout brothers were beheaded and surrendered their pure and righteous souls to Christ Whom they loved even unto death. Vassa tearfully thanked God for accepting her boys into His kingdom and for counting them worthy to receive the crowns of martyrdom. She knew that, although her sons were now at peace in God's Kingdom, her own struggle had not yet ended.

Thrown into prison with nothing to eat or drink, Vassa prayed. The compassionate and merciful God heard her prayer and sent His angel to feed her and to strengthen her in her agony.

Soon Vicarius set out for Macedonia and commanded Vassa to follow him. He had not yet finished with his attempts to force her into paganism, and she would provide a special challenge for him on his journey. He tried various means—water, fire, stoning—yet with each affliction he devised, an angel came to her aid and delivered her.

As they entered a nearby city, Vassa was forced to enter a pagan temple. The pious Christian prayed to God and, fortified with prayer, knocked over a huge idol with her own hands, shattering it into small pieces. The pagans were greatly enraged that she had profaned their gods and demanded that she be thrown to the wild beasts. Again, God spared the devoted mother, and the animals did not harm her.

"Throw this woman into the sea!" Vicarius ordered. He had tried to kill her in many different ways but nothing would end her life. The order was carried out and Vassa was thrown into the sea. But this time, to the amazement of all, she was seen sitting upon a throne being carried away by three men brighter than the sun.

Eight days later, after Vassa was discovered on Alon, a small island near the Hellespont, the consul of the area arrested her. Refusing once more to sacrifice to the idols, she was beheaded. The faithful Christian mother who had bravely endured so much entered her heavenly home where she took her place with her sons before the glorious throne of God.

Saint Christodoulos

n Patra, Greece, during the first decades of the nineteenth century, lived a young man named Christodoulos who had witnessed the martyrdom of Saint Anastasia, a young Christian maiden. At the time, Greece was occupied by the Moslem Turks who sought every opportunity to slaughter Orthodox Christians who would not deny their faith.

One day fourteen-year-old Christodoulos was seized and taken before Yousouf, the Turkish pasha who underestimated the young boy's great faith and courage. Since Christodoulos had witnessed the tortures and martyrdom of a Christian, Yousouf assumed that the boy would cower easily under pressure, deny Christ and accept Mohammed.

But young Christodoulos fearlessly stood before the pasha and boldly shouted, "Christos Anesti!" ("Christ is risen!") Yousouf became wild and immediately ordered that the lad be given five hundred lashes that were to continue for fourteen days—a day of torture for each year of the boy's life. The brave, young Christian remained firm in his faith and in his love for the Lord and, despite his torments, chanted hymns to his only Master, Jesus Christ. Loudly enough for all to hear, he shouted, "My body may belong to you, but my soul belongs to God Whom I will never abandon!" Having said these words, Christodoulos, the pious young Christian, joyfully surrendered his pure soul to God and took his place among the righteous children of the Lord.

Bibliography

Arianzou, Bishop Joseph, "Chinese Glory." Thessalonica, Greece: Orthodox Kypseli Publications, 1999.

Balan, Arch. Ioanichie. Romanian Patericon, Saints of the Romanian Orthodox Church, vol. I. Forestville, CA: St. Herman of Alaska Brotherhood, St. Paisius Abbey, 1996.

Charkiewicz, Yaroslaw. "In Poland, A Second Pascha." http://www.roca.org/oa/118/118h.htm

Demetrios, Saint of Rostov. The Great Collection of the Lives of Saints, vols. 1-3. Translated by Fr. Thomas Marretta. House Springs, Missouri: Chrysostom Press, 1994, 1995, 1997.

Ford, David and Mary. Marriage as a Path to Holiness, Lives of Married Saints. South Canaan, PA: St. Tikhon's Seminary Press, 1994.

Holy Apostles Convent, trans. The Lives of the Holy Women Martyrs. Buena Vista, CO: Holy Apostles Convent, 1991.

Makarios, Hieromonk of Simonos Petra. The Synaxarion, The Lives of the Saints of the Orthodox Church, vols. 1&2. Translated by Christopher Hookway. Ormylia: Holy Convent of the Annunciation of Our Lady, 1998-1999.

Markish, Mark. "Stars of the Orient, In Memory of the New Martyrs of China." www.chinese.orthodox.ru/ENGLISH/stars_e.htm

Migne, J.P. Patrologia Graeca. vol. 114, Symeon Logothetou (Metaphrastes), book 1. Paris: Apus Garnier Fratres, 1903.

Moses, Monk of the Holy Mountain. Married Saints of the Church. Translated by Ryassaphore-Nun Melania Reed and Ryassaphore-Nun Maria Simonsson. Wildwood, CA: St. Xenia Skete, 1991.

Orthodox America. "Child Saint of Poland—Martyr Gabriel of Zabludov." www.roca.org/oa/71/71h.html

Orthodox Church of America. "Feasts and Saints of the Orthodox Church," Dec. 29/Jan. 11. "The Holy Martyred 14,000 Infants." www.oca.org/pages/orth_chri/Feasts-and-Saints/Dec-29.html

Orthodox Church of America. "Feasts and Saints," Feb. 6. "The Holy Virgin Martyress Fausta." www.oca.org/pages/orth_chri/Feasts-and-Saints/Feb-06.html

Orthodox Church of America. "Feasts and Saints," www.oca.org/pages/orth_chri/Feasts-and-Saints/Jun-15.html

Orthodox Metropolitanate of Hong Kong and Southeast Asia. "The Feast of the Chinese Martyrs." Reprinted from "The Censer" by OCMC Magazine; vol. 15, No.2 www.ocmc.org/magazine/1999ii/1999ii-08.html

Papadopoulos, Leonidas J. and Georgia Lizardos and others, trans. New Martyrs of the Turkish Yoke. Seattle, Washington: St. Nectarios Press, 1985.

Velimirovic, Bishop Nikolai. The Prologue from Ochrid, vols. 1-4. Translated by Mother Maria. Birmingham, England: Lazarica Press, 1985, 1986.

Ἀλεξίου, Ἀρχιμ. Ἰωάννου. Οἱ Νέοι στὸ Μαρτύριο. Ἀθῆναι, Ἀδελφότης Θεολόγων ἡ «Ζωή», 1990

Γαλανοῦ, Μιχαὴλ Ι. Οἱ Βίοι τῶν Ἁγίων τοῦ Μηνολογίου τῆς Ὀρθοδόξου Ἑλληνικῆς Ἐκκλησίας, τόμοι 1-4. Ἀθῆναι· Ἀποστολικὴ Διακονία, 1999.

Νικοδήμου Ἁγιορείτου. Συναξαριστὴς τῶν Δώδεκα Μηνῶν τοῦ Ἐνιαυτοῦ, τεῦχοι Α´ καὶ Β´, Ἰωαννίνων· Πάνου Θεοδοσίου, 1819.

Νικοδήμου Ἁγιορείτου. Συναξαριστὴς τῶν Δώδεκα Μηνῶν, τόμοι Α´-ΣΤ´. Θεσσαλονίκη· «Ὀρθόδοξος Κυψέλη», 1993, 1998.

Ὁ Μάρτυρας τῶν Κατακόμβων, ἔκδοσις Χριστιανικὴ Ἐλπίς. Θεσσαλονίκη, 1987.

Σωτήρχου, Π.Μ. Παιδιομάρτυρες. Ἀθῆναι· Ἐκδοτικὸς Οἶκος «Ἀστήρ», 1995.

Index of Proper Names

Glory be to God
for all things.